AS IT IS IN

HEAVEN

AS IT IS IN

HOW ETERNITY BRINGS FOCUS

HEAVEN

TO WHAT REALLY MATTERS

GREG LAURIE

A NavPress published resource in alliance
with Tyndale House Publishers, Inc.

NavPress is the publishing ministry of The Navigators, an international Christian organization and leader in personal spiritual development. NavPress is committed to helping people grow spiritually and enjoy lives of meaning and hope through personal and group resources that are biblically rooted, culturally relevant, and highly practical.

For more information, visit www.NavPress.com.

ISBN 978-1-61291-569-2

Cover design by Faceout Studio, Jeff Miller
Cover image by Shutterstock #100119578 (Petr Malyshev)

Created and compiled in association with Stan Guthrie

Some of the anecdotal illustrations in this book are true to life and are included with the permission of the persons involved. All other illustrations are composites of real situations, and any resemblance to people living or dead is coincidental.

Unless otherwise identified, all Scripture quotations in this publication are taken from the Holy Bible, English Standard Version® (ESV®), copyright © 2001 by Crossway, a publishing ministry of Good News Publishers. ESV® Text Edition: 2011. Used by permission. All rights reserved. Other versions used include: the New American Standard Bible® (NASB), copyright © 1960, 1962, 1963, 1968, 1971, 1972, 1973, 1975, 1977, 1995 by The Lockman Foundation, used by permission; the *Holy Bible, New International Version*® (NIV®). Copyright © 1973, 1978, 1984, 2011 by Biblica, Inc.® Used by permission of Zondervan. All rights reserved worldwide. www.zondervan.com. The "NIV" and "New International Version" are trademarks registered in the United States Patent and Trademark Office by Biblica, Inc.®; the Holy Bible, New Living Translation (NLT), copyright © 1996, 2004, 2007 by Tyndale House Foundation, used by permission of Tyndale House Publishers Inc., Carol Stream, IL 60188, all rights reserved; and the King James Version (KJV).

Laurie, Greg.
  As it is in heaven : how eternity brings focus to what really matters / Greg Laurie.
      pages cm
  Includes bibliographical references and index.
  ISBN 978-1-61291-569-2 (alk. paper)
  1. Heaven--Christianity. 2. Future life--Christianity. I. Title.
  BT846.3.L38 2014
  236'.24--dc23
                                    2013038183

Printed in the United States of America

19   18   17   16   15   14
7   6   5   4   3   2

CONTENTS

1. MUCH ADO ABOUT HEAVEN 7
2. LIFE IS THE WARM-UP ACT 19
3. THE MAN FROM HEAVEN 31
4. A HOPEFUL HEAVEN 43
5. FLYING OVER HEAVEN 55
6. WHAT HEAVEN KNOWS ABOUT EARTH 67
7. WHEN SEEING IS BELIEVING 79
8. HEAVEN'S MESSENGERS 91
9. HEAVEN'S HEROES 103
10. A ROYAL CHEERING SECTION 113
11. PARTY TIME 125
12. IN THE TWINKLING OF AN EYE 137
13. HERE COMES THE JUDGE 149
14. HEAVEN'S REWARDS 163
15. CHRIST'S RESURRECTION — AND OURS 173
CONVERSATION GUIDE 183
NOTES 245

CHAPTER 1

MUCH ADO ABOUT HEAVEN

Have you ever seen that show on television called *Inside the Actor's Workshop*? On this program, which has been around since 1994, all kinds of celebrities get to talk about their craft. But even more interesting to me is that they get to share their personal life philosophies. At the end of every program, interviewer James Lipton asks his guests a series of questions:

1. What is your favorite word?
2. What is your least favorite word?
3. What turns you on?
4. What turns you off?
5. What sound or noise do you love?
6. What sound or noise do you hate?
7. What is your favorite curse word?
8. What profession other than your own would you like to attempt?
9. What profession would you not like to do?

These questions are great for getting real insight into a person's thinking and character. You can use them at parties, in small group Bible studies, or even as a way to break the ice in personal evangelism. But I think that Lipton saved his best question for last. Here it is:

10. If Heaven exists, what would you like to hear God say when you arrive at the pearly gates?[1]

The answers run the gamut. Here are a few (paraphrased) that have stuck with me over the years:

- Ben Affleck: "Your friends are in the back. They are expecting you."
- Ellen Barkin: "Come in. Have a drink. Sit down. Smoke a cigarette."
- Angelina Jolie: "You are allowed in."
- Johnny Depp: "Wow."
- Richard Dreyfuss: "Come in. It is not as boring as you might have thought."
- Anthony Hopkins: "What were you doing down there?"
- Will Smith: "Good work, Dog."
- Robert Redford: "You are too early."
- Tom Cruise: "Come on in. You did a good job."
- Susan Sarandon says what *she* will say to *God*: "Let's party."
- Robert De Niro, for his part, says, "If Heaven exists, God has a lot of explaining to do." (That is one of my favorites. *Really?* A lot of explaining to *Robert De Niro?* I wonder if the Lord would look at De Niro and say, "What? Are you looking at *Me*?")
- James Lipton (responding to his own question): "See, Jim, you were wrong."

Our culture, supposedly so fixated on getting ahead in the here and now, is fascinated with Heaven and the afterlife, but I probably didn't even need to tell you that. You can see it for yourself. According to one public opinion survey by the Gallup organization,[2] 81 percent of Americans believe in Heaven (while a smaller share, 69 percent, believes in Hell).

According to LifeWay Research and *Christianity Today*, 33 percent of Americans who never attend worship services wonder, at least some of the time, whether they will get to Heaven. Forty-three percent of born-again or evangelical Protestants ask themselves that question, while 66 percent of liberal or mainline Protestants do. Amazingly, 64 percent of young people aged eighteen to twenty-nine wonder whether they will get to Heaven. Even in the supposedly secular Northeast, a full 69 percent of people surveyed have questioned whether they will go to Heaven when they die.[3]

Type "Do you believe you are going to Heaven or Hell?" into Google and you will get a variety of quizzes and answers from instant experts. Wiki.answers.com, Quizrocket.com, Patheos.com, Answers .yahoo.com, and many more will all endeavor to tell you — or help you find the answer for yourself. And let's face it, if the *Web* tells you where you will end up in the afterlife, it must be true!

Movies about Heaven abound. One of my favorites is *It's a Wonderful Life*, a 1946 classic starring Jimmy Stewart, who plays George Bailey, a good but tortured man who attempts to kill himself because his life seemingly has fallen apart. On the night of George's suicide attempt, Heaven sends him Clarence Odbody (played by Henry Travers), a man who has died and is trying to "earn his wings" as a bumbling angel. It's a great story, but the theology is odd, to say the least! Then there is *Ghost*, a 1990 film starring Patrick Swayze and Demi Moore. Swayze's character is murdered, but he loves Moore so much that he comes back to earth as — you guessed it — a ghost. And you can choose from *two* movies called *Heaven Can Wait*, one from 1947 starring Gene Tierney and Don Ameche, and another from 1978 starring Warren Beatty and Buck Henry.

The classic *Star Trek* television series and movies, of course, mixed in lots of references to Heaven, a "Paradise lost" by mankind, and God. While the franchise didn't always get these serious subjects right amid all the science fiction and pop psychology, I have to give it an A for effort. For example, in *Star Trek II: The Wrath of Khan* — the one in which the funeral music for Spock is "Amazing Grace" — early on the philosopher James T. Kirk tells a young Vulcan officer, "How we deal with death is at *least* as important as how we deal with life, wouldn't you say?" *I* sure would!

Heaven is a major theme in American business, too. If you go to Amazon.com and type in the word Heaven, you will be confronted with more than 200,000 options, ranging from books to music to other things that you can purchase about the subject. I'm talking about Heaven-themed T-shirts, wristbands, food, gambling opportunities, and so on. Lots of people hope to earn some treasure here on earth by selling something pointing to our hoped-for treasure in Heaven.

Then there are the books (including this one). While the afterlife is of perennial reading interest — think *The Weight of Glory* and *The Screwtape Letters* by C. S. Lewis, for example — the subject got a huge boost with books by doctors reporting on the so-called near death experiences, or NDEs, of their patients. Elisabeth Kübler-Ross wrote the ground-breaking book, *On Death and Dying*, which describes the five stages of grief. However, she is just as well-known for her book, *On Life After Death*, which summarizes her study of 20,000 NDEs. The work had a profound effect on Kübler-Ross, who died in 2004. At one point she said, "I've told my children that when I die, to release balloons in the sky to celebrate that I graduated. For me, death is a graduation."[4]

A whole train of books followed the example of Kübler-Ross. In 1975, Dr. Raymond Moody released a book called *Life After Life*, which describes the author's investigation of one hundred cases where people had been pronounced clinically dead. We've all heard the stories of people who "died" in their hospital rooms, had a sensation of floating above their bodies on the hospital bed, could see and hear everything that went on around them, eventually went through a dark tunnel, emerged to speak with a calming "being of light," and were eventually sent back. The details are remarkably similar across these cases. Author Dinesh D'Souza notes that Plato, the ancient Tibetan *Book of the Dead*, and even Ernest Hemingway have spoken of this kind of phenomenon.[5]

Some of today's bestselling books are written by people purporting to tell us about their experiences of dying and going to Heaven. One is *90 Minutes in Heaven*, by Don Piper, who "died" in a car crash. "In my next moment of awareness, I was standing in Heaven," Piper says. "Joy pulsated through me as I looked around, and at that moment I became aware of a large crowd of people. They stood in front of a brilliant, ornate gate. I have no idea how far away they were; such things as distance didn't matter. As the crowd rushed toward me, I didn't see Jesus, but I did see people I had known. As they surged toward me, I knew instantly that all of them had died during my lifetime. Their presence seemed absolutely natural."[6]

Another is *Heaven Is for Real*, by Todd Burpo. It tells the story of three-year-old Colton Burpo, who barely survived an emergency appendectomy. Months later, when riding with his family past the same hospital in North Platte, Nebraska, Colton nonchalantly told his mother, "That's where the angels sang to me."[7] Soon his parents—as well as a large chunk of the American reading public—heard the child's detailed descriptions of Heaven and what went on there.

And just to assure you that these accounts are not the fevered imaginings of a few religious wackos, I'll mention just one more popular volume. It's called *To Heaven and Back: A Doctor's Extraordinary Account of Her Death, Heaven, Angels, and Life Again*, by Mary C. Neal. She is an orthopedic surgeon, specializing in the human spine. In 1999 Neal drowned in a kayaking accident in Chile. She, too, had an NDE.

"It was as though I was experiencing an explosion of love and joy in their absolute, unadulterated essence," Neal writes in her book.[8] Now I am not in a position to say if these people have or have not gone to Heaven. I don't know if they just made this stuff up, if they are mistaken, or if they indeed had some time in the next dimension. I don't know, and none of us really can know. All we can do is take what they write and compare it to what is in Scripture, because the Bible is a trustworthy guide to everything we need to know about Heaven—as well as to our lives here on earth. Yes, we will take a little bit of time in this book to interact with what some of these friends say about their heavenly experiences, but our answers about Heaven will be found in the pages of the Bible. I don't have to go beyond what's in that book.

And trust me, when you see what God's Word says about this incredible topic, I think you'll agree that we're in for an exhilarating journey — both now and, ultimately, in eternity.

But the book you hold in your hands — or on your e-reader — is not simply another description of what the Bible teaches about Heaven, though it would be well worth your time if that's all it did. And indeed, I'll keep you supplied with more than enough facts, verses, and Scripture references to keep you, your small group, and your friends informed on the vital topic of Heaven. But we have lots of good books like that already, and those who are interested in this topic know where to get them.

This book is a little bit different, in my humble opinion. Most books about Heaven rightly get us to think about what lies beyond in, as Hamlet soliloquized, the "undiscovered country." They try to get us to Heaven, but they seem to be lacking a little bit in getting us back home. This one, I hope, will get you to think about how Heaven makes a difference for our life on earth — right here, right now. The title gives it away, I think: *As It Is in Heaven: How Eternity Brings Focus to What Really Matters*. The unique angle of this book is that what goes on in Heaven can really provide us with practical direction and inspiration right now.

You see, God is not only interested in the "bye and bye." He is also interested in the "here and now."

At this point, lots of people might say, "So what? I'm a busy person with lots of interests and responsibilities. I don't have time to think about sitting on a cloud and strumming a harp. I'll take care of earth, and I'll let God take care of Heaven (if there is one)." I understand that viewpoint — understand, but don't agree! What goes on in Heaven is not like some obscure theological topic, like how many angels can dance on the head of a pin — and I doubt seriously that we could talk even one angel into doing something so ridiculous, anyway! Trust me; they've got much better things to do!

Yes, there *are* clouds in Heaven, but no one is sitting on them! Heaven will not be a boring place, eternally unrelated to what goes on here on Planet Earth—far from it. *Excitement* is too poor a word to capture the depth, the pleasure, and the significance of heavenly realities, but Heaven *will* be exciting. We know this because of the testimony of God's Word and the testimony of God's people who have gone before us.

In this volume, you will discover what these believers already in Heaven are focused on. When you do, you will find your passion to reach the lost and establish a spiritual legacy renewed, your sense of determination in prayer reinvigorated, your faith in the King of kings rekindled, and your passion and compassion for the plight of the persecuted Christians stronger than ever. In this book, I will give you stories, principles, and practical applications for the great truths of Heaven and what difference they make right now. Friend, excitement beyond anything you've experienced is yours once you catch a clear glimpse of Heaven.

Eternity, you see, brings clarity to what really matters in time. Here are some of the questions we'll take a look at:

- Are people in Heaven watching us or are they too occupied with worshiping God to pay attention?
- How will our perspective change when *we* are in Heaven?
- What do people in Heaven remember about life on earth?
- What can we learn from what the Bible says is going on there right now?

Here's where we're headed:

Chapter 2: Life Is the Warm-Up Act. Knowing what Heaven is about helps us understand what life on earth is about. If you want to know the meaning of life, read on!

Chapter 3: The Man from Heaven. Jesus Christ came from Heaven to tell us how to get there. Who did He say He was, what evidence is there that He was right, and what must we do to enjoy eternal life—both now and forever?

Chapter 4: A Hopeful Heaven. As you get older, people you know will die, and Heaven will become more and more compelling to you. The hope of reunions with believing loved ones is real, has a long history, and is a great spur to our faith.

Chapter 5: Flying over Heaven. What does the Bible say about Heaven, the dwelling place of God? What are we going to do there? This chapter shows how we will see His face, worship Him, and carry significant responsibilities for the kingdom.

Chapter 6: What Heaven Knows About Earth. What do people in Heaven know about what is going on here on earth? Do they care about us? Are they perhaps watching us right now? In this chapter, we'll learn that people in eternity have a new set of priorities and values, as a very poor man on earth finds himself in the place of comfort and peace, while a rich man ends up in torment and anguish.

Chapter 7: When Seeing Is Believing. A picture is worth a thousand words, but what about an up-close and personal view from the throne room of Heaven? What do the saints see clearest now that they are in Heaven with Christ?

Chapter 8: Heaven's Messengers. Angels are "ministering spirits" who protect, deliver, guide, and bring messages from God to His elect. You don't need to engage them, and you don't need to try to communicate with them. Just step back and let them do their jobs.

Chapter 9: Heaven's Heroes. While the persecution of Christians for the sake of the gospel rarely, if ever, makes headlines here on earth, it will be all the buzz in Heaven.

Chapter 10: A Royal Cheering Section. Chapters 11 and 12 of Hebrews tell us that people in Heaven are crying out to the Lord on our behalf, perhaps cheering us on in the race of faith. Having dealt with every imaginable trial of faith themselves, they are intent on our progress as we "look to Jesus."

Chapter 11: Party Time. When people on earth believe in Jesus, it is public knowledge in Heaven, and its inhabitants break out in celebration. Do we? Or are we so preoccupied with the here and now that we fail to echo the chorus of heavenly praise?

Chapter 12: In the Twinkling of an Eye. The Rapture of believers into Heaven is the next great event on the prophetic calendar. It could happen at any moment. Who gets to go, and what difference should it make in our lives today?

Chapter 13: Here Comes the Judge. The default setting for every person is not Heaven. Judgment is real, and it is coming. This chapter will tell you who goes to Hell, why, and how to avoid this awful fate.

Chapter 14: Heaven's Rewards. Heaven is a place where we rest from our labors. It is also a place where we are *rewarded* for those labors. Over and over, the Bible promises that we will be rewarded in Heaven. What might those rewards look like?

Chapter 15: Christ's Resurrection — and Ours. Heaven is a wonderful blessing, but it has an expiration date. The Bible tells us that a "new heaven and a new earth" are coming. We are not only given eternal life, but we are destined for resurrected, bodily life.

As I said, this is going to be an exciting, life-changing journey. To get us started and to whet our appetite, I want us to look at a key passage. It's from the Lord's Prayer, when Jesus' disciples asked Him how to pray.

Our Father in Heaven,
hallowed be your name.
Your kingdom come,
your will be done,
    on earth as it is in heaven.
Give us this day our daily bread,
and forgive us our debts,
    as we also have forgiven our debtors.
And lead us not into temptation,
    but deliver us from evil. (Mt. 6:9-13)

If you're like me, you have heard or read this prayer hundreds, if not thousands, of times. But I want you to notice something you may have missed. In verse 10, where we are to pray for God's will to be done "on earth as it is in heaven," have you ever stopped to consider what it means for God's will to be done *in Heaven*, and how we are to emulate and work for God's will right here on terra firma? My job is not to get *my* will in Heaven; it is to get *God's* will on earth. One thing is for sure: People in Heaven are already doing God's will, and we are called to do the same thing.

We're going to cover this subject throughout the pages of this book, but right now let's just take a quick look at some key verses that spell out what God's will for His children is. Matthew 6:10 reminds us that, except for the fact that we face different circumstances, God's will for us here on earth is the same as it is for Christians who have already moved on to Heaven. So these verses will give us real insight into what matters for Christians, "on earth as it is in heaven."

- John 7:17: "If anyone's will is to do God's will, he will know whether the teaching is from God or whether I am speaking on my own authority." Desiring God's will, Jesus says, is something we should aspire to.
- Romans 15:32: "So that by God's will I may come to you with joy and be refreshed in your company." God's will is to bring Christians together for their refreshment.
- 1 Peter 3:17: "For it is better to suffer for doing good, if that should be God's will, than for doing evil." Though there is no suffering in Heaven, there are questions about it. God sometimes allows the suffering of His faithful saints for His own purposes.
- Psalm 40:8: "I delight to do your will, O my God; your law is within my heart." God's people delight in doing God's will, on earth and in Heaven.
- Luke 22:42: "Father, if you are willing, remove this cup from me. Nevertheless, not my will, but yours, be done." We ought to desire, as Jesus did, to do God's will, whether we are in Heaven or on earth.
- Ephesians 5:17: "Therefore do not be foolish, but understand what the will of the Lord is." God's will for us can be known, and we are to seek it, even as it is known in Heaven.

- 1 Thessalonians 5:16-18: "Rejoice always, pray without ceasing, give thanks in all circumstances; for this is the will of God in Christ Jesus for you." Isn't this a brief description of what Heaven looks like?
- Hebrews 13:20-21: "Now may the God of peace who brought again from the dead our Lord Jesus, the great shepherd of the sheep, by the blood of the eternal covenant, equip you with everything good that you may do his will, working in us that which is pleasing in his sight, through Jesus Christ, to whom be glory forever and ever. Amen." In Heaven or on earth, we are to be equipped "with everything good" in order to do His will. On earth we do this imperfectly, ever seeking to perform God's will "as it is in heaven."

So we see in these verses that what God desires for us on earth is a precursor to what awaits us in Heaven. What is already (and perfectly) happening *there* ought to affect us *here*. Sometimes it is said that some people are so heavenly minded that they're no earthly good. That saying has always bothered me. Isn't it true, rather, that some people are so *earthly* minded that they're no *heavenly* good? Perhaps we could also say that some people are so *earthly* minded that they're no *earthly* good. While we think pursuing our earthly lives is the most important thing to bring peace and prosperity to the planet, God is telling us that we need to pursue heavenly priorities in order to do the most earthly good.

That makes a lot of sense, doesn't it? A focus on Heaven is very practical—perhaps the most practical focus we can have. In his book *Who Is This Man?*, John Ortberg describes the outsized influence of the Man of Galilee, who died on a Roman cross two millennia ago. "Normally when someone dies, their impact on the world immediately begins to recede," Ortberg says, yet "Jesus inverted this normal human trajectory, as he did so many others."[9] Why is this? Certainly the beauty and power of His teachings constitute one reason, but let's remember that when He died, His followers were disconsolate. They thought it was all over. But something changed their perspective on the third day—Christ's resurrection from the grave. Glimpsing Heaven, they became a joyous company that began to turn "the world upside down" (Acts 17:6). An earthly focus can only take us so far. We need to see eternal things. Such a focus not only gives us peace and comfort. It empowers us to begin changing the world. Today.

So let's train ourselves to be heavenly minded and focus on eternity. It begins with a recognition that the meaning of our lives on earth is to be found in Heaven.

CHAPTER 2

LIFE IS THE WARM-UP ACT

One day an older man was speaking to a student about his plans. He asked the young man, "Tell me, what are your plans after you graduate from law school?"

The young man said, "Well, I would like to get a job with a good firm and start making some money."

The older guy said, "All right. Sounds good. Then what?"

"Well, then I would like to get married."

"All right. Then what?"

"I would like to start a family, have some children, put my kids in good schools, and have enough money to eventually get a second home."

"Okay. Then what?"

"After I have worked for a while, maybe I could come to a point where I would retire. Then, if my health were good, my wife and I could travel around the world."

"Then what?"

"Well, maybe we would have grandchildren. You know, I have heard that grandchildren are more fun than children."

The older man said, "That's true. But then what?"

"Well, I guess I would pass my money on to my children, hoping that they will have as comfortable of a life as I have had."

"Yes. Then what?"

"Well," the young man said, "I guess I will die."

And the older man said, "Yes. Then what?"

Then what? "Then" is eternity. Far too often we think of this life as being everything. Unless we get bad news from the doctor or a loved one dies, we seldom give thought to the next life. But the reality is, what we call "life" is actually the *before life*. Then comes the *afterlife*. What we are experiencing now is sort of like the warm-up act.

Eternity! Eternity!
How long art thou. Eternity?
A little bird with fretting beak
Might wear to naught the loftiest peak,
Though but each thousand years it came;
Yet thou wert then, as now, the same.
Ponder, O man, eternity![1]

There is more to come, much more. Though vanishingly short in comparison with eternity, however, this life is still of utmost importance, because it sets the stage for all that is to come. This is another reason we are to pray for the Father's will to be done on earth "as it is in heaven." If we live as citizens of Hell during our pitiful threescore and ten years under the sun, we cannot expect to be welcomed as citizens of Heaven after we die. What we do down here *matters*, and in fact it sets our course for our eternity — for good or for ill.

Remember this: The choices of time are binding for eternity. Yes, eternity matters, and therefore so does our life right now.

So here is the $64,000 question. Why do we exist? Why are we here on this earth? Why did God create us in the first place? And where do we find the answer? It's funny where some people will look.

I have an iPhone. It has a "personal voice assistant" called Siri that will answer any question you have. Just push the button and say, "Siri, where can I get a good cup of coffee?" And Siri will use a navigational device to figure out where you are before presenting you with a bunch of establishments that sell coffee near you.

So the other day, I pulled out my iPhone and asked Siri, "Siri, what is the meaning of life?" The answer: "I can't answer that right now, but give me a long time to write a play in which nothing happens." So I pressed the button again. "I don't really know," came the answer, "but I think there is an app for that." I pressed it again. "All evidence to date points to chocolate." (Someone very clever must be writing this material!) I pushed it again. "I am surprised you would ask that question of an inanimate object." Exactly.

But Siri's answers are no worse than those from a lot of other sources. In one poll of Americans, 61 percent said the main purpose of life is enjoyment and personal fulfillment.[2] Now we might expect that from nonbelievers. But 50 percent of those who claim to be born-again Christians said that life's purpose is enjoyment and self-satisfaction. Is that true? Do we really exist merely for personal enjoyment and self-satisfaction?

To find the answer, we have to go to Scripture. In effect, we must go to Heaven to find out why we are here on the earth. And that is exactly where an amazing scene unfolds before us in Revelation 4:1:

> I looked, and behold, a door standing open in heaven! And the first voice, which I had heard speaking to me like a trumpet, said, "Come up here, and I will show you what must take place after this."

John the apostle has been banished to the island of Patmos "on account of the word of God and the testimony of Jesus" (Rev. 1:9). In the first part of Revelation, John receives an overview of the seven churches of Asia (1:9–3:22), starting with Ephesus and ending with Laodicea. Now, however, he is hurtled into the next dimension and sees things that are yet to come. John is trying to use the language of his day to describe what is before his eyes.

And what does he see?

> At once I was in the Spirit, and behold, a throne stood in heaven, with one seated on the throne. And he who sat there had the appearance of jasper and carnelian, and around the throne was a rainbow that had the appearance of an emerald. Around the throne were

twenty-four thrones, and seated on the thrones were twenty-four elders, clothed in white garments, with golden crowns on their heads. (Rev. 4:2-4)

Now, we don't know who the elders are. Some think they may be the twelve patriarchs from the Old Testament and the twelve apostles from the New. Others think they may just be believers who have been given this exalted position for their faithful service. The point is, they are *people*.

And then the scene changes rapidly. John sees ominous storm warnings from the throne of God (see 4:5). Trouble is coming to Planet Earth. Next, John sees some angelic creatures.

The four living creatures, each of them with six wings, are full of eyes all around and within, and day and night they never cease to say,

"Holy, holy, holy, is the Lord God Almighty,
    who was and is and is to come!" (4:8)

Then the heavenly worship service grows:

Whenever the living creatures give glory and honor and thanks to him who is seated on the throne, who lives forever and ever, the twenty-four elders fall down before him who is seated on the throne and worship him who lives forever and ever. They cast their crowns before the throne, saying,

"Worthy are you, our Lord and God,
    to receive glory and honor and power,
for you created all things,
    and by your will they existed and were created." (4:9-11)

These twenty-four elders cast their crowns before God's throne. He is "worthy," they say, "for" (or because) He is Creator. God is worthy of our worship because He created us. It's as simple as that, and yet maybe not so simple. The elders add another reason — "by your will they existed and were created." I like the way the King James Version puts verse 11: "Thou art worthy, O Lord, to receive glory and honour and power: for thou hast created all things, and for thy pleasure they are and were created."

Did you catch that? According to these elders, we exist to bring God glory and pleasure. *That is the meaning of life.* It is something your iPhone will never tell you. We exist to bring God glory and pleasure. Now if that's true, then we have to face another simple fact: We don't exist to bring *ourselves* glory and pleasure. So no matter what 61 percent of Americans — or even 50 percent of born-again Christians — might say, the main purpose of life cannot be seeking our own enjoyment and personal fulfillment.

In fact, if I live for pleasure, I will never find it. Let me repeat that: If I live for pleasure, I will never find it. The Bible says in 1 Timothy 5:6 that "she who is self-indulgent is dead even while she lives."[3] The fact of the matter is that self-indulgence, living for pleasure, is one of the least pleasurable things a person can do. In fact, it has been said that the best cure for hedonism is an attempt to practice it. I believe it.

Freddie Mercury was the lead singer of the rock band Queen, which has sold between 150 million and 300 million records. Members of this group, needless to say, were awash in cash and fame. They had it all. And Mercury had the opportunity, as few ever have had, to devote his life to the pursuit of pleasure. In fact, one of his friends, Elton John, said that Mercury was the only person who could out-party him. Mercury's appetites were unquenchable. In an interview, he was quoted as saying, "Excess is a part of my nature. To me dullness is a disease. I need danger and excitement. . . . Straight people bore me stiff. I love freaky people."[4]

Mercury did not deny himself anything . . . sexually or materially. But it didn't turn out well. And it never does. He realized that in his attempt to be a star, he had effectively created a monster. He later said, "The monster is me. Success, family, money, sex, drugs, whatever you want I can have it. But now I am beginning to see that as much as I created it I want to escape from it. I am starting to worry that I can't control it as much as it controls me."[5] Mercury lost his fight with the monster. He died from complications due to AIDS at the age of forty-five.

The pursuit of pleasure apart from God is indeed a monster. When God saw trouble developing in the heart of Cain, the Lord issued him a warning. Here is my paraphrase of Genesis 4:7: "Sin is lying at your door like a crouching beast. Its desire is for you, but you should rule over it." Sin is like a crouching beast ready to pounce on you — ready to control you — and if you live for pleasure, that beast is going to take over.

So living for pleasure will never bring pleasure. The writer of Ecclesiastes, who called himself the Preacher, discovered this for himself.

> I said in my heart, "Come now, I will test you with pleasure; enjoy yourself." But behold, this also was vanity. I said of laughter, "It is mad," and of pleasure, "What use is it?" I searched with my heart how to cheer my body with wine — my heart still guiding me with wisdom — and how to lay hold on folly, till I might see what was good for the children of man to do under heaven during the few days of their life. I made great works. I built houses and planted vineyards for myself. I made myself gardens and parks, and planted in them all kinds of fruit trees. I made myself pools from which to water the forest of growing trees. I bought male and female slaves, and had slaves who were born in my house. I had also great possessions of herds and flocks, more than any who had been before me in Jerusalem. I also gathered for myself silver and gold and the treasure of kings and provinces. I got singers, both men and women, and many concubines, the delight of the sons of man.
>
> So I became great and surpassed all who were before me in Jerusalem. Also my wisdom remained with me. And whatever my eyes desired I did not keep from them. I kept my heart from no

pleasure, for my heart found pleasure in all my toil, and this was my reward for all my toil. Then I considered all that my hands had done and the toil I had expended in doing it, and behold, all was vanity and a striving after wind, and there was nothing to be gained under the sun. (Eccl. 2:1-11)

Freddie Mercury had *nothing* on the Preacher! They both sought out every pleasure imaginable. And both discovered that a focus on earth and self will never satisfy. We were made for God and Heaven, not simply for life "under the sun." As the Preacher admitted, God "has put eternity into man's heart" (Eccl. 3:11). C. S. Lewis longed for something just on the edge of his spiritual vision, something hinted at in nature or in the best stories but always just beyond his grasp. Lewis finally discovered that he was longing for Heaven.

Yet there is something paradoxical about all this. Even though we cannot gain lasting pleasure by pursuing it, by living for *God* we will experience real pleasure—not by seeking *it*, but by seeking *Him*. The Bible says that in His presence there is fullness of joy and at His right hand are pleasures forevermore (see Ps.16:11).

The key to a full and joyful life on earth is a heavenly focus on the glory of God. Here are some verses to support that contention:

- Isaiah 43:7: "Everyone who is called by my name, whom I created for my glory, whom I formed and made."
- Ephesians 1:11 tells us that God chose us from the beginning that we should bring forth praise to our glorious God.
- 1 Corinthians 6:19 says, "Do you not know that your body is a temple of the Holy Spirit within you, whom you have from God? You are not your own."
- 1 Corinthians 10:31: "Whether you eat or drink, or whatever you do, do all to the glory of God."

So here is my question for you: Are you living for God's glory, or are you living for your own? You should be able to write over any pursuit, "Hallowed be *Thy* name." Can you write that over your marriage right now? Over your career and business ethics? Over what you fill your leisure time with? "Hallowed be Thy name." Are you living for the glory of God?

As we have seen, life is preparation for eternity. Life is the warm-up act. We were made *by* God and *for* God. And God wants us to practice on earth what we will do forever in eternity. And what is that? Revelation 5:1-11 has the answers:

I saw in the right hand of him who was seated on the throne a scroll written within and on the back, sealed with seven seals. And I saw a mighty angel proclaiming with a loud voice, "Who is worthy to open the scroll and break its seals?" And no one in heaven or on earth or under the earth was able to open the scroll or to look into it, and I began to weep loudly because no one was found worthy to open the scroll or to look into it. And one of the elders said to me, "Weep no more; behold, the Lion of the tribe of Judah, the Root of David, has conquered, so that he can open the scroll and its seven seals."

And between the throne and the four living creatures and among the elders I saw a Lamb standing, as though it had been slain, with seven horns and with seven eyes, which are the seven spirits of God sent out into all the earth. And he went and took the scroll from the right hand of him who was seated on the throne. And when he had taken the scroll, the four living creatures and the twenty-four elders fell down before the Lamb, each holding a harp, and golden bowls full of incense, which are the prayers of the saints. And they sang a new song, saying,

"Worthy are you to take the scroll
     and to open its seals,
for you were slain, and by your blood you ransomed people for God
     from every tribe and language and people and nation,
and you have made them a kingdom and priests to our God,
     and they shall reign on the earth."

Then I looked, and I heard around the throne and the living creatures and the elders the voice of many angels, numbering myriads
of myriads and thousands of thousands.

A seven-sealed scroll was an extremely important document in the
ancient world. The wills of the Roman emperors Vespasian and Caesar
Augustus were secured with seven seals. A scribe would get out a long
roll of parchment and start writing. After a while, he would stop, roll
the parchment enough to cover his words, and seal the scroll at that
point with wax. Then he would write again and seal and repeat until
finished. This would ensure that the scroll would be read a portion at
a time. You would have to break open the seal. Read. Break open the
next seal. Read some more. Break open the next seal. Keep reading.

In this heavenly scene, everyone is weeping because no one is
worthy to open the scroll, which I believe is the title deed to the earth.
By the way, while it's true there is no crying in Heaven, caught up in
this powerful vision, John was weeping profusely. He wept because the
world is under the sway of the Devil (see 1 Jn. 5:19), and there seemed
to be no deliverance. But then the "Lamb of God, who takes away the
sin of the world" (Jn. 1:29) arrives and takes the scroll. The scene suddenly erupts in worship.

Let's remember that one of the great pastimes of Heaven is worship
of the Lord. That is why we ought to get practicing right now. Note
Revelation 5:8: "And the twenty-four elders fell down before the Lamb,
each holding a harp, and golden bowls full of incense, which are the
prayers of the saints." Not only does God keep our tears in a bottle (see
Ps. 56:8), He also keeps our prayers in a bowl. The point is, God never
throws them away. He stores them. Some prayers are answered right
away. Others are kept in heavenly storage for an answer to come later.

We all know there are times when life just doesn't seem fair. Things
happen that don't make sense. And we say, "Well, why did God not
answer my prayer?" This scene encourages us to believe He will answer
our prayers in His way . . . for His glory . . . in His time.

I think when we are in Heaven, standing before God's throne, and that golden bowl full of prayers is brought before us, we will realize that God heard every little prayer. We are going to realize that His answer was far better than what we asked for in a particular moment. What we don't grasp in our hardships or tragedies is how they fit together with other events in our lives to touch people, who will in turn have an impact on someone or something else, and so on, and so on. Long chain reactions are going to produce this, that, and the other thing for His glory. In the meantime, we are going to have to trust Him. It is all going to be revealed in Heaven when we stand before the Lord.

So everyone breaks out in adoration in this heavenly scene. It is a global praise service from every dimension:

> "Worthy is the Lamb who was slain,
> to receive power and wealth and wisdom and might
> and honor and glory and blessing!"
>
> And I heard every creature in heaven and on earth and under the earth and in the sea, and all that is in them, saying,
>
> "To him who sits on the throne and to the Lamb
> be blessing and honor and glory and might forever and ever!"
>
> And the four living creatures said, "Amen!" and the elders fell down and worshiped. (Rev. 5:12-14)

Again, God wants us to practice on earth what we will do forever in eternity. And what is that? It is the worship and the glorification of God. That is why I am here. That is why we are here—for His pleasure. And as we do His will, paradoxically, we will find our own deepest needs being met. That's how we were created. The Westminster Shorter Catechism has it right when it says, "Man's chief end is to glorify God, and to enjoy him forever."[6]

Remember the conversation that Jesus had with the woman at the well in John 4? This woman had been married and divorced five times and was living with a man at the time. Jesus says to her, "If you drink of this water you will thirst again." He used that well as a metaphor for life. "Let me tell you something, Lady," He was saying. "Men are never going to fill the deepest need of your life. That is why you have gone back to the well five times. You will always thirst. But if you drink of the water I give, you will never thirst again." We must turn from our earthly worship of self to a heavenly worship of Him. God is a Spirit, He said, and those who worship Him must worship Him in spirit and in truth. And then He said that God is looking for people to worship Him. To see clearly why we were put on this earth, we must take our eyes off ourselves.

Even today, God is looking for people who will get this, who will understand the reason they are here. If you live for pleasure, you will never find pleasure. You will be like the woman at the well . . . drinking, drinking, but never satisfied. "I am going to have this experience. I am going to chase after something else now. I am going to pursue the monster."

Look at what happened to Freddie Mercury. What a waste of a life created in God's image. Mercury is just one sad example. So many people chase after the wind and throw their lives away, seeking answers from their iPhones rather than from God's sure Word. But if you put God and heavenly priorities first, I can assure you that you will find the reason for which you were created.

Of course, if we want to know what Heaven values, it only makes sense to learn from the Man who came from Heaven. Who was He, why did He come to earth, and what did He say about the heavenly kingdom and how to get there?

CHAPTER 3

THE MAN FROM HEAVEN

Once Natalie Portman was asked about the afterlife. "I don't believe in that," the actress said. "This is it, and I believe it's the best way to live."[1]

George Clooney said, "I don't believe in happy endings, but I do believe in happy travels, because ultimately, you die at a very young age, or you live long enough to watch your friends die. It's a mean thing, life."[2]

William Shatner, once the dashing young Captain Kirk in the original Star Trek television series, is an octogenarian now, and he's not so sure about what awaits him in the afterlife. "I'm so not ready to die," he said in an interview. "It petrifies me. I go alone. I go to a place I don't know. It might be painful. It might be the end. My thought is that it is the end. I become nameless, and I spent a lifetime being known."[3]

It's amazing how often we look to celebrities in our culture for insight or information about really important issues. And what could be a more important issue than our eternal destiny? Celebrities perhaps have no special insight on this topic, although they certainly may reflect and even shape popular views. So perhaps we should seek out the views of others. We've already taken note of contemporary American opinion about Heaven, and yet maybe relying on opinion polls is not the best way to get reliable information about the afterlife, either.

Perhaps we ought to look not at our contemporaries, but to our forebears. Now it's true that we Americans are biased toward whatever is new and against what is old. This is because our scientific worldview, handed down to us from the Enlightenment, tries to tell us that things are always getting better. We are always getting smarter, so of course we weren't as smart back in the day, the argument goes. Therefore, any insight or argument from the past is automatically suspect. C. S. Lewis called this kind of bias "chronological snobbery."

The present has no future, however, if it doesn't listen to the past. Roman philosopher Cicero said, "History is the witness that testifies to the passing of time; it illumines reality, vitalizes memory, provides guidance in daily life and brings us tidings of antiquity."[4] So maybe those who have gone before us can tell us what we need to know about the afterlife. Certainly belief in the afterlife is not unique to our time. Almost every culture, past and present, believes in something beyond the grave.

- Archaeologists have discovered a five-thousand-year-old boat in an Egyptian tomb. The Pharaoh was to use it to sail the Heavens into the next life.
- The ancient Greeks would often place a coin in the mouth of a corpse so he could pay the fare to cross the River Styx.
- American Indians would bury a pony and a bow with arrows along with a dead warrior so that he could ride into the happy hunting ground.
- Norsemen would bury a dead hero's horse with him so he could ride proudly into the afterlife.
- The Romans believed that the righteous would picnic in the Elysian Fields with their horses grazing nearby.
- Eskimos of Greenland who died in childhood customarily were buried with their dogs, who were to guide them through what was believed to be the cold wasteland of death.

These peoples had many different conceptions of what awaits us after death, although they agreed that people had to be *prepared* to make the journey to the other side. You couldn't just show up. You had to pay the fare, or bring your own transportation. Whether the authority for these directions came from the *Egyptian Book of the Dead*, the *Epic of Gilgamesh*, or some other source, there were always instructions that had to be followed . . . to the letter.

Of course, most of us don't take these claims literally anymore, perhaps because of our own chronological snobbery. Some of us will listen instead to a psychic, read about a near death experience, or concoct our own pet theories. However, others will look to their own religious traditions for wisdom and solace.

While all of these sources of information may be intriguing, wouldn't it be better to have the eyewitness testimony of someone who has actually *been* in Heaven? Certainly this is one reason why the growing number of books by people who claim to have been to the other side is such a publishing phenomenon. And yet many of these accounts do not agree, either with each other, or with established religious teaching. How do we decide what is true?

Well, in ordinary life, if I want to know about something, I ask an expert. An expert can be someone who knows lots of facts about a subject through years of study. We have many "experts" of this nature, even when it comes to what the afterlife might be like. Yet this kind of expert won't do the trick for us if we want to really *know* about Heaven, because he or she hasn't really *been* there. We need another kind of expertise — personal experience. When we want to go on a vacation somewhere new, we'll likely consult travel books. But if we're smart, we'll also talk to someone with firsthand knowledge. "Tell me about this place," we might ask. "You were born there." That is the kind of expertise we need when thinking about Heaven.

According to Jesus, there *is* life beyond the grave. Many religious figures have said the same. So why should we accept *His* word over the word of another? Put simply, the answer is this: Jesus is the only one who came from Heaven. And besides that, He has returned to Heaven. That is why Christ and Christ alone can address this topic with authority. He is an eyewitness to heavenly Reality.

"For I have come down from heaven," Jesus said in John 6:38, "not to do my own will but the will of him who sent me." In other words,

Jesus did what He has told us to do—do God's will here on earth as it is in Heaven. Jesus, unlike any other religious figure past or present, knew God the Father's will in Heaven because He was there with Him. He was from there. He was a native.

While Jesus' followers called Him Lord, Son of God, Master, and Teacher, Jesus liked to call Himself the "Son of Man." On one level, this title hearkened back to the prophet Ezekiel, who was called "son of man" by God many times, to emphasize His humanity. But on another level, this self-designation pointed to Christ's deity.

When the religious authorities demanded to know from Jesus whether He was the Messiah and Son of God, Jesus answered affirmatively, "You have said so. But I tell you, from now on you will see the Son of Man seated at the right hand of Power and coming on the clouds of heaven" (Mt. 26:64). He was quoting Daniel 7:13-14, in which "one like a son of man . . . was given dominion and glory and a kingdom, that all peoples, nations, and languages should serve him." According to Jesus' own words, He was (and is) both human and divine. If Jesus carried a business card, "Heaven" would probably be on it somewhere!

"No one has ascended into heaven," Jesus said to Nicodemus, "except he who descended from heaven, the Son of Man" (Jn. 3:13). Jesus' authority on the subject of Heaven therefore is unique.

But how do we know Jesus wasn't simply deluded or lying about His connection with Heaven? Maybe He just got caught up in an excess of religious enthusiasm. Many Christian apologists, of course, have referenced the argument by C. S. Lewis:

> A man who was merely a man and said the sort of things that Jesus said would not be a great moral teacher. He would either be a lunatic—on a level with the man who says he is a poached egg—or else he would be the Devil of Hell. You must make your choice.[5]

Even Bono, the lead singer of U2, chimes in with a similar statement about who Jesus Christ was.

Look, the secular response to the Christ story always goes like this: he was a great prophet, obviously a very interesting guy, had a lot to say along the lines of other great prophets, be they Elijah, Muhammad, Buddha, or Confucius. But actually Christ doesn't allow you that. He doesn't let you off that hook. Christ says: *No. I'm not saying I'm a teacher, don't call me teacher. I'm not saying I'm a prophet. I'm saying: "I'm the Messiah." I'm saying: "I am God incarnate."*[6]

I think I am on solid ground in making my choice: Jesus is who He said He is, and He is where He said He is — in Heaven. On the morning He was physically resurrected from the tomb, Jesus told an astonished Mary Magdalene, "I am ascending to my Father and your Father, to my God and your God" (Jn. 20:17). And indeed the disciples saw the resurrected Jesus ascend into Heaven forty days later (see Acts 1:9). Angels standing nearby told them that Jesus would come back "in the same way" (1:11).

The evidence for the physical, space-time resurrection of Jesus is an example of Heaven turning the old earthly order of sin and death upside down and inside out, ending the dreary reign of the second law of thermodynamics, which says that everything winds down, disintegrates, and falls apart. On earth, dead bodies don't normally regenerate; they decompose. Yet on the third day after the Crucifixion, Jesus rose from the dead. In this singular event, the power of Heaven overcame and reversed the power of earth. The Resurrection was a sudden triumph of Heaven over the forces of chaos. It provides a powerful body of evidence that Jesus was telling us the truth about Heaven.

But how do we know that the numerous New Testament accounts of Christ's resurrection aren't mere religious fantasy and wishful thinking from gullible, pre-scientific rubes? Well, there are numerous books that examine the Resurrection as a historical event. Since *this* is a book about Heaven and we need to stay on track, we'll just touch lightly on this topic.

Dinesh D'Souza notes the incredible transformation that the disciples underwent after the Crucifixion. The most obvious explanation for their newfound courage is that they were eyewitnesses to the Resurrection — because Jesus didn't stay dead.

> The disciples became so convinced of what they had seen that their dirges of lamentation were replaced with cries of joy. Proclaiming Christ crucified and Christ risen, they launched the greatest wave of religious conversion in history. The number of Christians increased from around one hundred at the time of Christ's death to around thirty million by the early fourth century, when emperor Constantine himself converted to Christianity. These conversions occurred in the teeth of fierce opposition and the persecution of the greatest empire of the ancient world, the empire of Rome. The early Christians did not hesitate to identify themselves with a man who had been branded a traitor and a criminal. They endured imprisonment, torture, exile, and death rather than renounce their commitment to a resurrected Christ.[7]

World-class scholar N. T. Wright has written a monumental work that examines the historical evidence for the resurrection of Jesus Christ called *The Resurrection of the Son of God*. After carefully weighing and sifting all of the evidence, Wright asserts near the end of his massive tome:

> We are left with the secure historical conclusion: the tomb was empty, and various "meetings" took place not only between Jesus and his followers (including at least one initial skeptic) but also, in at least one case (that of Paul; possibly, too, that of James), between Jesus and people who had not been among his followers. I regard this conclusion as coming in the same sort of category, of historical probability so high as to be virtually certain, as the death of Augustus in AD 14 or the fall of Jerusalem in AD 70.[8]

So now let's move on to some intriguing statements about Heaven from the Man who was there to see what difference Heaven ought to make in our lives today. Then we will see what this Man said about how we are to actually get to Heaven ourselves. After all, knowledge about Heaven does us no good if we don't have the right to live there for eternity ourselves.

> The same day Sadducees came to him, who say that there is no res-urrection, and they asked him a question, saying, "Teacher, Moses said, 'If a man dies having no children, his brother must marry the widow and raise up offspring for his brother.' Now there were seven brothers among us. The first married and died, and having no off-spring left his wife to his brother. So too the second and third, down to the seventh. After them all, the woman died. In the resurrection, therefore, of the seven, whose wife will she be? For they all had her."
>
> But Jesus answered them, "You are wrong, because you know neither the Scriptures nor the power of God. For in the resurrection they neither marry nor are given in marriage, but are like angels in heaven. And as for the resurrection of the dead, have you not read what was said to you by God: 'I am the God of Abraham, and the God of Isaac, and the God of Jacob'? He is not God of the dead, but of the living." And when the crowd heard it, they were astonished at his teaching. (Mt. 22:23-33)

In the time of Jesus, many Jews had an aberrant view of the after-life. One group, the Sadducees, might be described as theological lib-erals. They did not believe what the Bible says about a coming judgment or an afterlife. They only accepted the five books of Moses—Genesis, Exodus, Leviticus, Numbers, and Deuteronomy—as being inspired by God. Because these books do not explicitly teach about a resurrec-tion of the dead, they did not believe in one. It was a bleak worldview. So in our story they come to Jesus, hoping to provoke Him with a "gotcha" question that they think illustrates the absurdity of the doc-trine: "In the resurrection, . . . whose wife will she be?"

Even so, their absurd question calls for an answer about marriage in Heaven, and Jesus gives one, as someone who has been there. "You are wrong," He says, "because you know neither the Scriptures nor the power of God. For in the resurrection they neither marry nor are given in marriage, but are like angels in heaven" (Mt. 22:29-30). So the Bible teaches that there is no marriage in Heaven. Right? Not quite. There will be marriage in Heaven, but it will be a marriage between Jesus Christ and His bride, the church:

> "A man shall leave his father and mother and hold fast to his wife, and the two shall become one flesh." This mystery is profound, and I am saying that it refers to Christ and the church. (Eph. 5:31-32)

> Then came one of the seven angels who had the seven bowls full of the seven last plagues and spoke to me, saying, "Come, I will show you the Bride, the wife of the Lamb." (Rev. 21:9)

That's great, you may be thinking, but what about our marital relationships on earth? Marriage, of course, has specific functions here on earth, namely, the propagation of the human species and the creation of oneness between a husband and wife (see Gen. 1:28; 2:24-25). Marriage on earth is incredibly special, but it is limited to this world. In Heaven, of course, there will be no need to propagate, and the love of husband and wife will be transcended by an inestimably purer love for our Creator. We will not be losing something (marriage), so much as we will be gaining something far greater (the wonderful blessing of being with God in the company of our loved ones). Randy Alcorn says, "Earthly marriage is a shadow, a copy, an echo of the true and ultimate marriage. . . . The purpose of marriage is not to replace Heaven but to prepare us for it."[9]

So, no, we won't be married to each other as we are now. Our primary relationship will be with God. But we will still be connected to each other, related to one another. In fact, our relationships will even be stronger. "On Earth," Alcorn says, "the closer we draw to him, the closer we draw to each other. Surely the same will be true in Heaven."[10]

In a parallel account of Jesus and the Sadducees, Jesus says that "those who are considered worthy of taking part in the age to come and in the resurrection from the dead will neither marry nor be given in marriage, and they can no longer die; for they are like the angels. They are God's children, since they are children of the resurrection" (Lk. 20:35-36, NIV).

People sometimes have strange ideas about the afterlife. Some folks believe that we become angels, perhaps based on this passage. You sometimes hear people say, "Well, God needed another angel in Heaven." No. An angel is a created being made by God Himself. Men and women don't *become* angels. Jesus here says people related to God by faith are *like* angels, raised for a new life.

Having cleared up the Sadducees' misconceptions about marriage, Jesus moves in to clinch the argument about the afterlife. Rather than attempt to convince the Sadducees that their own crabbed doctrine concerning Scripture is off the mark, He allows the battle to be waged on what they think is their own turf—on the Pentateuch, the five books of Moses.

He quotes from Exodus, where God says He "is" the God of the three great patriarchs—Abraham, Isaac, and Jacob. The Lord's argument turns on a verb tense. The Exodus quote does not say that God "was" their God, but that He "is" their God. God is the great *I Am*. He is the God not of the dead, but of the living. The conclusion: The patriarchs, though departed from this world, are still alive. The point: A believer never dies.

In fact, we need to grasp an even bigger truth, according to Jesus: *Everyone* is immortal. Everyone lives forever. I don't care who you are. You are a believer. You are a nonbeliever. You are an agnostic. You are an atheist. You live forever. Every Christian. Every Buddhist. Every Hindu. Every Muslim. Every person. Every Republican. Every Democrat. Even lawyers live forever!

So you say, "That is good news that I won't stop existing." At this point, maybe William Shatner would breathe a sigh of relief. But another question determines whether your eternal existence is actually good news or not.

Where will you live forever?

Let's say that I bought you a one-way plane ticket. It entitles you to a first-class seat. You get excited and start packing. But you ought to look at the ticket before you get too enthusiastic. If it says your destination is Siberia in January, I wouldn't get too terribly excited. That is *not* where you want to go. But if it says Maui, your eagerness will be fully justified.

So the issue is not, "Am I going to live forever?" as much as it is "*Where* am I going to live forever?" And according to the Bible, there are only two places—Heaven or Hell. So what happens to Christians when they die? They go straight to Heaven. No stopovers. When I book a flight, I always try to avoid stopovers. Well, let me assure you that it is a direct flight to Heaven. The moment a believer takes a final breath on earth, he or she will take his or her first breath in Heaven. And after that, the believer will go into the presence of God.

Remember that Jesus said to the thief on the cross, "Truly, I say to you, *today* you will be with me in Paradise" (Lk. 23:43, emphasis added). Paul, who was converted through an encounter with the risen Christ, told the Philippians, "My desire is to depart and be with Christ, for that is far better" (Phil. 1:23). He didn't say, "I am going to depart and then go into a state of suspended animation or soul sleep or Purgatory or have a stopover in Detroit," or something like that! No. He says, "I will depart and be with Christ." He also affirmed in 2 Corinthians 5 that he preferred to be away from the body and at home with the Lord.

This is the hope of every follower of Jesus Christ—to be with Him one day in Heaven. But we don't go to Heaven to find Christ. He can be with us now! We go to Christ to find Heaven. Jesus died on the cross to pay the penalty for our sin and was raised so that those who trust in Him will have eternal life with Him in Heaven—starting right now. As Jesus said, "Truly, truly, I say to you, whoever believes has eternal life" (Jn. 6:47). According to Jesus, Heaven starts for us the moment we place our faith in Him.

But Jesus also had something disturbing to say concerning the afterlife. Tragically, everyone's destination is not Heaven. "Enter by the narrow gate," the Lord solemnly warned. "For the gate is wide and the way is easy that leads to destruction, and those who enter by it are many. For the gate is narrow and the way is hard that leads to life, and those who find it are few" (Mt. 7:13-14). Which gate are you going through?

If you want to fly somewhere right now, you can't just drive to the airport and walk onto a plane. You wouldn't even get *that* far. You would be stopped in security. "Where is your ticket?" you would be asked. "Where is your boarding pass? Let me check your ID. Take off your shoes."

In the same way, you need to pay the fare to get to Heaven. Unfortunately, the cost is far more than you could ever afford. But the good news is that at the cross Jesus Christ died for you and purchased your ticket. He offers it to you as a gift. *Right now.*

It is a gift we should neither despise nor neglect. Those who receive it will enjoy unending happiness. Those who reject it, as revealed either in their words or actions, face unending torment. The choice is yours.

In Matthew 25, Jesus urges watchfulness until His return, for the free offer of Heaven will not last forever. After the parable of the ten virgins, he says, "Watch therefore, for you know neither the day nor the hour" (v. 13). After the parable of the talents, the Lord warns, "For to everyone who has will more be given, and he will have an abundance. But from the one who has not, even what he has will be taken away. And cast the worthless servant into the outer darkness. In that place there will be weeping and gnashing of teeth" (vv. 29-30). And following the frightening description of the Last Judgment, He says, "And these will go away into eternal punishment, but the righteous into eternal life" (v. 46).

Someone once asked the great evangelist D. L. Moody, "If you knew the Lord was returning tonight, how would you spend the rest of your day?" Moody replied, "I wouldn't do anything different than I do every day."[11] That is how every Christian ought to live. Can you say that today?

Heaven needs to affect how we live on this earth. We have this truth on the authority of the Man from Heaven.

CHAPTER 4

A HOPEFUL HEAVEN

My beautiful mother wanted to look like Marilyn Monroe. She never hugged me, she never told me she loved me, and she went out a lot. I saw her rarely. Sometimes she would come and make an appearance, and I would be so excited to see her, and then she would disappear again. This was the cycle of my life. Being with her. Not being with her. Dealing with all of the things she went through as an alcoholic and as someone who married and divorced seven times. And then I was sent to the Southern California Military Academy on Signal Hill in Long Beach.

The home of my grandparents, whom I called Mama Stella and Daddy Charles, where I lived much of the time, had a portrait of Christ hanging on the wall. As a little boy, I would look at it and feel great admiration for Him. I would think, "I wish I could know this Jesus. But He came. He died. He is gone or maybe He is up there somewhere. I don't know where and I don't know how to communicate with Him."

Though my life had taken a lot of difficult twists and turns, in 1970 I heard a message about Christ that I understood, and I prayed and asked Him to come into my life. From that moment on, things started turning for the better. I was determined to not follow in the footsteps of my mother. Though she had been married seven times, *I* was going to have a successful marriage. So after I met and married Cathe, we were committed to doing everything possible to make our marriage strong. Then our first son came along, Christopher, followed, ten years later, by Jonathan. And because I never had a father growing up, *I* wanted to be a hands-on father, a loving father, a *present* father. I wanted to teach them the way of the Lord . . . but I wanted to have fun with them, too.

Christopher was precocious, always getting into trouble — but we always loved him with all of our hearts, and he knew it. In his twenties, he rebelled against the Lord. Cathe and I discovered that he was living a double life, drinking and partying away.

So we prayed and endured many sleepless nights. And then God got ahold of Christopher, and he made a recommitment to Christ. He got married to a wonderful girl named Brittany, and in time our first granddaughter, little Stella (named after her grandmother), was born.

Next, little Lucy was on the way.

But my life changed on July 24, 2008. It was a sunny day. Not a cloudy day. Not a rainy day. We were at home. Cathe was doing a Bible study with Brittany and her mom. I was watching Stella. We hadn't heard from Christopher. He was on his way to our church, where he worked. We tried to call him. He didn't answer. So I texted him: "Where are you?" There was no answer. We soon found out why: My son left this world around 9:01 a.m. in an automobile crash.

I had served as a pastor for quite a long time and had actually been with parents when they heard this kind of news. I have seen the devastation up close and personally, and I wondered how I would react if such news were to ever darken my doorstep.

It was too horrible a thought to contemplate, and I consoled myself by saying, "That will never happen to me. I've already suffered enough in life."

Well, it did happen to me, and when I heard the horrific news that I would never see my son again on this earth, time just stopped. I went into an immediate state of shock. I could not stand . . . and collapsed on the floor. I don't even know if I cried. I was, however, able to get up.

Soon, our home was filled with well-wishers, but I had to get away. I escaped to my office, which is over our garage, fell on the floor, and cried out to God for help, not to get through the day, but through the minutes. It was a nightmare from which I kept hoping I would wake.

Well, it has been years since that terrible day. I am still mourning. It still hurts. Is it the same as it was back then? No. It isn't. It is different. Is it better? In a way. We have received the Lord's comfort in so many ways. But there is still a gaping hole in our lives that was once occupied by Christopher. I have learned how to live with pain. I have become a part of a club I never wanted to join. Hardly a day goes by when I don't encounter someone who has also lost a loved one and who is asking for some kind of help. And perhaps through God's grace, Cathe and I have been able "to comfort those who are in any affliction, with the comfort with which we ourselves are comforted by God" (2 Cor. 1:4).

It's been said, "If you preach to hurting people, you will never lack for an audience." I have found that to be true. And there certainly are a lot of hurting people out there, and I am one of them.

However, I want to tell you something else I have come to understand. I have learned about hope—and I have hope. It is actually more real than it has ever been for me. From the valley of the shadow of death, I have found the hope promised in Scripture. The Lord says, "For I know the plans I have for you, declares the Lord, plans for welfare and not for evil, to give you a future and a hope" (Jer. 29:11).

Now, of course, that promise was first given to the Israelites in Babylonian captivity. Because of their idolatry, the Lord had banished them to idolatrous Babylon for seventy long years. Despite all that, God was still saying, "Israel, listen to me. Your days are *not* over. I have a future for you." And He is saying the same to us who have put our faith in Jesus Christ.

The word translated here as *future* could be better translated as *an expected end*. Another translation would say *a ground of hope* or *things hoped for*. In other words, there will be an outcome. There will be completion in your life. God will tie up the loose ends.

God, the premier Artist, is working on a canvas. That canvas is you. Day by day He adds to it, with a line here, a bit of shading there, a splash of color another time. Impatiently you say, "Wow, Lord, what is that going to be? Finish it. Come on. Complete it." But He just keeps painting in His own time. In God's mind, of course, the art is done. The painting is completed. In the same way, God looks at you, still a work in progress in time, but knows exactly where you are headed. For Him, it's a done deal.

Now sometimes people will say to those of us in mourning, "Well, you shouldn't be crying. You shouldn't be in mourning. This loved one is in Heaven." I understand this perspective, because there is an element of truth in it if the one who died is a believer. An entrance into Heaven is worth celebrating, and we will look at this later in the book. But even the apostle Paul confronted deep sorrow when contemplating the death of a friend. In Philippians 2 he talks about how a fellow laborer for the gospel, Epaphroditus, had almost died. "But God had mercy on him," Paul says, "and not only on him but on me also, lest I should have sorrow upon sorrow" (v. 27). Remember, Paul had been to Heaven and back. And yet he is admitting that he doesn't know whether he could have borne it if Epaphroditus had died.

And that is how it can feel. You wonder, *Can I get through this?* It's natural. The Bible says there *is* a time to weep and a time to mourn (see Eccl. 3:4). Friend, please don't ever tell a person who has lost someone to get over it or to stop crying. I think of some things that I have flippantly said even to people who were going through a time of mourning. I had their best interests in mind. I meant well, but I didn't really know what I was talking about. We need to give such people space and time. Mourning is part of the healing process. Let's be patient with people who are in grief.

But now let me say a word to you who are mourning the loss of someone. You need perspective. Psalm 42 provides some:

> My tears have been my food
>   day and night,
> while they say to me all the day long,
>   "Where is your God?"
> These things I remember,
>   as I pour out my soul:
> how I would go with the throng

and lead them in procession to the house of God
with glad shouts and songs of praise,
> a multitude keeping festival. (vv. 3-4)

I know what the psalmist means when he says, "My tears have been my food"—when you have a breakfast, lunch, and dinner of tears. And you lose your appetite. And you cry constantly.

It's not like normal crying or even weeping.

It's more like you have a knife in your stomach, and you can hardly breathe.

You sob so deeply you wonder if you will ever stop.

Cathe told me she had only seen me cry maybe two or three times in our life together. But after the Lord took Christopher, I cried every day, for hours. Deep crying. Sometimes I still go into emotional black holes where there is seemingly no light.

But then the psalmist corrects himself:

Why are you cast down, O my soul,
> and why are you in turmoil within me?
Hope in God; for I shall again praise him,
> my salvation and my God. (vv. 5-6)

He's preaching to *himself*! I have learned to do the same thing. When I get depressed about Christopher, I will tell myself, "Greg, you listen to me. The Bible says you will see your son again. He is in Heaven. And the Bible says that Jesus is the resurrection and the life and he that believes in Him will not die." Someone overhearing me would think I am a lunatic. And maybe I am. But I am a hopeful lunatic! Then I will remind myself of other promises of God—about the peace He gives, about His presence, and so on. I will quote them out loud to myself. While this practice isn't magic, it usually lifts me from an emotional pit. We all need to do this from time to time, so don't be shy about it. God's Word can give us hope even in the darkest days.

John 11 is an account of people who have lost hope. It is a story of the death of a loved one, a story to which I can really relate. Mary, Martha, and Lazarus are a tightly knit family. These siblings love each other, and they have a great home. Mary, Martha, and Lazarus can legitimately say that Jesus of Nazareth is their friend because He frequently visits their home in Bethany. But now tragedy strikes.

> A certain man was ill, Lazarus of Bethany, the village of Mary and her sister Martha. It was Mary who anointed the Lord with ointment and wiped his feet with her hair, whose brother Lazarus was ill. So the sisters sent to him, saying, "Lord, he whom you love is ill." (vv. 1-3)

Lazarus was ill. I don't know why, but some of us think we are going to somehow make it through life unscathed. Without a major tragedy. No illness. Never a lost loved one. And then when something bad comes our way, as it must, we are shocked. Don't be shocked. After all, remember 1 Peter 4:12: "Beloved, do not be surprised at the fiery trial when it comes upon you to test you, as though something strange were happening to you." Don't be surprised. Don't ask why it's happening. It happens to everyone. Jesus said, "In the world you will have tribulation" (Jn. 16:33).

It's going to come. It is going to knock at your door. It may start with your grandparents. And then your parents. Eventually it could be your spouse. It might be a child. Maybe it will be a close friend to remind you of your own mortality.

And notice what these sisters say in John 11:3: "Lord, he whom you love is ill." They knew Jesus loved them. The word used here for love is from the Greek word phileo, for brother love. "Lord, the friend you love like a brother is sick." That was the word that they sent to Jesus. That is the perfect thing to do when crisis hits — bring it to Jesus.

Notice the basis for their appeal. They didn't say, "Hey, Lord, you owe us. We fed you all the time." They just said, "Lord, the one whom you love is sick." They based their appeal not on their love for God but rather on *His* love for them. Why? Because God's love for us is consistent and never-changing.

Yet something strange is about to happen:

> When Jesus heard it he said, "This illness does not lead to death. It is for the glory of God, so that the Son of God may be glorified through it."
>
> Now Jesus loved Martha and her sister and Lazarus. So, when he heard that Lazarus was ill, he stayed two days longer in the place where he was. (Jn. 4-6)

Yet notice something else from these verses. God loves us. Don't rush over that. God loves us. Let it sink in. God loves *you*. Listen to this: Whatever He does or allows in your life as His child is motivated by His everlasting love for you. God says in Jeremiah 31:3, "I have loved thee with an everlasting love: therefore with lovingkindness have I drawn thee" (kjv). He loves you. And He loved Mary, Martha, and Lazarus.

Instead of rushing right over and performing the cure, Jesus waits. Why? Interestingly, when Jesus chooses a Greek word for love, it is not *phileo*, or brother love, but *agape*, which speaks of God's all-consuming love. And Jesus, because He loved Lazarus in this way, does not come when they wanted Him to come.

Remember, His delays are not necessarily His denials. Just as surely as God has His will, He has His timing. Jesus is trying to help Mary and Martha get the big picture: *I know it seems as if I should come there right now, but I am going to go above and beyond your request. Just hang on.*

When the Lord finally shows up, Lazarus is not sick anymore. Lazarus is *dead* . . . and has been for four days. Decomposition has set in. Jesus not only did not *heal* His friend. He even missed the funeral. Imagine how these sisters felt.

Seeing Him come down the road, Martha is going to give Jesus a piece of her mind:

> So when Martha heard that Jesus was coming, she went and met him, but Mary remained seated in the house. Martha said to Jesus, "Lord, if you had been here, my brother would not have died. But

even now I know that whatever you ask from God, God will give you." Jesus said to her, "Your brother will rise again." Martha said to him, "I know that he will rise again in the resurrection on the last day." Jesus said to her, "I am the resurrection and the life. Whoever believes in me, though he die, yet shall he live, and everyone who lives and believes in me shall never die. Do you believe this?" (Jn. 11:20-26)

Pretty brash words from Martha. But notice this: She wasn't running from Jesus. She was running *to* Jesus with her problems. We need to do the same. Tell God when things don't seem to make sense. He knows your heart anyway. And remember that Jesus cried out from the cross, "My God, My God, why have You forsaken Me?" (see Psalm 22; Matthew 27). He was calling on His Father. Don't withdraw from God and from your Christian friends. Go to the Lord and cry out to Him. Ask why. You probably won't get an answer (Job didn't), but go ahead and ask. He will listen.

Jesus doesn't give Martha an explanation, but He does put things into an eternal perspective. "Your brother will rise again." "Yeah," she seems to be saying. "I know. In the resurrection. I have heard all that. Yes." "No," the Lord seems to be replying. "Read my lips. I am the resurrection and the life. He who believes in Me, though he were dead, yet shall he live. Whosoever lives and believes in Me shall never die."

Well, this seems to satisfy Martha. But now along comes Mary, asking the same tearful question: "Lord, if you had been here, my brother would not have died" (Jn. 11:32).

When Jesus saw her weeping, and the Jews who had come with her also weeping, he was deeply moved in his spirit and greatly troubled. And he said, "Where have you laid him?" They said to him, "Lord, come and see." Jesus wept. So the Jews said, "See how he loved him!" (11:33-36)

This scene reminds us that Jesus weeps with us in our time of pain. Yes, Jesus was God, with all power and glory. But He was also a man, a man who felt our pain and sorrows. As Isaiah 53:3-4 says,

> He was despised and rejected by men;
>   a man of sorrows, and acquainted with grief;
> and as one from whom men hide their faces
>   he was despised, and we esteemed him not.
>
> Surely he has borne our griefs
>   and carried our sorrows.

He knows. He voluntarily put Himself in the way of danger to bear our sorrows on the cross. Why? Hebrews 2:17-18 gives the answer:

> Therefore he had to be made like his brothers in every respect, so that he might become a merciful and faithful high priest in the service of God, to make propitiation for the sins of the people. For because he himself has suffered when tempted, he is able to help those who are being tempted.

Here's the takeaway. If something breaks *your* heart, it breaks *His* as well.

Look at verse 33 of John 11. "When Jesus saw her weeping, and the Jews who had come with her also weeping, he was deeply moved in his spirit and greatly troubled." The word for troubled could be better translated as mad. Yes, He is angry — ticked off, even. Why? Is He angry with the mourners — "What is wrong with you people?" Absolutely not. He feels complete compassion — He wept with them.

No. He is angry with the Grim Reaper, if you will. He is angry with death itself. This is not the way it was meant to be. There should have never been death in God's world. There should never have been aging, disability, sickness, or auto accidents. Death is an aberration. Death is not the way it was meant to be. But the Curse came because of the Fall, and Jesus was angry about that.

But now He is going to put God's glory on display in the midst of this tragedy. Jesus is not faking His tears and His anger. The death of Lazarus is real, but the power of God is even more real. Because of this, God can be glorified not only through healings and miraculous deliverances, but also *through* human suffering. He can bring good despite the bad.

In this case, Lazarus is raised from the dead. I feel kind of sorry for Lazarus. Honestly. If you could interview someone in Heaven and say, "Yeah, we were kind of thinking it would be good if you would go back to earth again, but we want to give you a choice," do you think he would go? That would be like trying to take a kid out of Disneyland who has been there for twelve minutes. But Lazarus had no choice. When Jesus calls, people answer.

Sometimes, then, God is glorified through the removal of the affliction. When you pray and it goes away, praise God. When the doctor operates and you are cancer free, praise God — and thank the doctor. These things are wonderful.

But then there are times when the surgery *doesn't* go as hoped. The illness is not removed. The problem is not taken away. And yet God can be glorified through our endurance. In the meantime, we develop hope through hardship.

> But we rejoice in our sufferings, knowing that suffering produces endurance, and endurance produces character, and character produces hope, and hope does not put us to shame, because God's love has been poured into our hearts through the Holy Spirit who has been given to us. (Ro. 5:3-5)

This hope reminds us that death is not all there is for those who love God. Physical death is not the end of existence. It is just a change in the state of our existence. The tomb is not the entrance to death, but the portal to life. Heaven is merely the earthly life of the believer glorified and perfected. When believers die, they go into God's presence in Heaven. That is the ultimate hope.

This truth is a source of profound hope for me and for others who have lost loved ones, of course. Back in the third century, Cyprian, bishop of Carthage, sought to encourage fellow believers who were facing severe persecution.

> We should consider that we have renounced the world, and in the meantime are living here as guests and strangers. Let us greet the day which assigns each of us to his own home, which snatches us from this place and sets us free from the snares of the world, and restores us to paradise and the kingdom. Anyone who has been in foreign lands longs to return to his own native land. . . . We regard paradise as our native land. Why do we not hasten and run, that we may behold our country, that we may greet our parents? There a great number of our dear ones is awaiting us, and a dense crowd of parents, brothers, children, is longing for us, already assured of their own safety, and still longing for our salvation. What gladness there will be for them and for us when we enter their presence and share their embrace![1]

Do you have that sure hope? If not, in what are you hoping? Some people hope in themselves. They are like Maria in *The Sound of Music*: "I have confidence in confidence alone." That won't get you very far when you die. Others put their hope in technology or in politicians. Hard to believe, but true!

Maybe you are facing a crisis right now. You didn't ask for it. You didn't expect it. But here it is. Maybe you have just heard the worst news imaginable. Maybe you are going through troubles in your marriage. Troubles at work. Troubles with your family. Physical troubles. Health troubles. Financial troubles. Reputation troubles. The list goes on and on. You are in anguish or anxiety right now. And you wonder, "*What* do I do?"

Here is what you do. You call out to God. He will hear you. And here is the great hope for the Christian. No matter what happens in life, we have His guaranteed assurance that when we die, we *will* go to Heaven.

This is the testimony, that God gave us eternal life, and this life is in his Son. Whoever has the Son has life; whoever does not have the Son of God does not have life. I write these things to you who believe in the name of the Son of God that you may know that you have eternal life. (1 Jn. 5:11-13)

You are either hopeful or hopeless. Proverbs 10:28 says, "The hope of the righteous brings joy, but the expectation of the wicked will perish."

Hope in God. Is Christ living inside of you? Do you *know* that you will go to Heaven when you die? If not, do you *want* this hope? You can find it right now.

In the next chapter, let's take a look at the big picture of Heaven, which is a key reason for our hope.

CHAPTER 5

FLYING OVER HEAVEN

One day, the story goes, a young Billy Graham was visiting a small town. He was there to preach in one of the churches. Before the service, he wrote a letter and wanted to send it to a friend, but he couldn't find the local post office. So Billy Graham saw a boy standing on a street corner and asked him. After the boy gave him the information, the great evangelist thanked him and, never one to miss an opportunity, invited the lad to the meeting.

"If you'll go to the church this evening," Billy Graham said, "you can hear me telling everyone how to get to Heaven."

"I don't think I'll be there," the boy replied. "You don't even know your way to the post office."[1]

Now, unlike many recent authors, I cannot claim to have been to Heaven. As a consequence, I might have as little credibility in describing the celestial abode as Billy Graham had with that little boy. You might be more inclined to trust what someone who claims to be an eyewitness says.[2] There is no shortage of vivid descriptions from self-proclaimed eyewitnesses that get our hearts racing.

Mary C. Neal, author of *To Heaven and Back*, says that after her kayaking accident, she and her companions "were traveling down a path that led to a great and brilliant hall, larger and more beautiful than anything I can conceive of seeing on earth. It was radiating a brilliance of colors and beauty."[3]

One day, Todd Burpo, father of Colton, was asking his son what he had seen when he had nearly died of appendicitis. "What do people look like in Heaven?" Todd asked.

"Everybody's got wings," the boy replied.

"Did you have wings?" Todd asked.

"Yeah, but mine weren't very big."

"Okay . . . did you walk places or did you fly?"

"We flew. Well, all except for Jesus. He was the only one in Heaven who didn't have wings. Jesus just went up and down like an elevator."[4]

Whatever we think of these kinds of contemporary accounts, even if they're all true, it's safe to say that they can only be vague approximations of the Reality. Alister McGrath tells the story of the great theologian Augustine of Hippo, who came upon a young boy who was scooping ocean water into his cupped hands and pouring it into a carefully dug hole in the sand, time after time. What, Augustine asked the boy, was he doing?

The child replied that he was putting the ocean into the hole. When Augustine said that this was impossible, the boy pointed out that it was no more impossible than what the theologian was attempting to do—describing God and heavenly realities in the pages of a book.[5]

Heaven has captured the imagination of human beings across the centuries, on every continent, and of many different faiths. Lisa Miller, the religion editor of *Newsweek*, writes that popular conceptions of Heaven have changed with the times.

To America, Puritans brought with them one kind of Heaven — austere and ominous—and that Heaven changed with the Civil War when 620,000 men died, leaving their daughters, wives, sisters, and mothers without fathers and husbands, brothers and sons. It changed again with the rationalism of the early twentieth century and again with the cataclysm of World War II. In America, we are heirs to all these conceptions: when thinking about Heaven, each of us unconsciously dips backward in time, we dabble, we enhance what we find there with our own histories, our own ideas of perfection.[6]

Yet whether we recognize it or not, there is a Reality behind all our conceptions—a Reality that judges all of them. That Reality is described accurately, though not exhaustively, in the pages of Scripture. The Bible is our surest guide to Heaven, because only it is completely trustworthy. And of course this matters supremely.

One day, perhaps sooner than we expect, Christians are going to be in Heaven and face that Reality firsthand. As we have seen, Jesus Christ came so that all who trust in Him and His finished work on the cross will go there, experiencing Heaven and God's love for eternity. Sadly, tragically, Heaven is not the destination of the nonbeliever. God desires everyone to be saved (see 1 Tim. 2:4), but if we choose to go our own way, He will give us our choice. As C. S. Lewis said, the doors to Hell are locked . . . on the inside. [7]

So what is Heaven like? What does Scripture say? In this chapter, we will do a flyover of Heaven, pointing out some of the most notable landmarks. Later in the book, we will zoom in for a closer look at what awaits us in the Celestial City.

Back in the sixties, Soviet cosmonaut Yuri Gagarin, who was the first man in outer space, was sent into orbit around the earth. "I see earth! It is so beautiful!" he said high above the planet. Yet his atheistic masters also quoted Gagarin as saying, "I looked and looked but I didn't see God."[8]

I'll tell you this much—had Yuri stepped out of that spacesuit, he would have seen God immediately! The bigger issue is, from a human perspective, we cannot see into the third Heaven. But that is the very dwelling place of God.

Now, wait a minute, you might be saying. We've been discussing Heaven, but what is this thing you call the "third Heaven"? Good question. The first thing we need to understand is that "third Heaven" is a biblical term. According to the Bible, there are three Heavens. Paul writes about that in 2 Corinthians 12:2-4:

> I know a man in Christ who fourteen years ago was caught up to the
> third heaven—whether in the body or out of the body I do not

know, God knows. And I know that this man was caught up into paradise — whether in the body or out of the body I do not know, God knows — and he heard things that cannot be told, which man may not utter.

The Bible assumes three Heavens. The first is the sky. Walk outside and look up at the expanse. What you see, and what you are breathing in, is the first Heaven. It consists of the atmosphere, which is home to the birds, the clouds, rainbows, and other atmospheric phenomena. The second Heaven includes everything in the cosmos beyond earth's atmosphere. The moon, the sun, the stars, the planets, and the galaxies all inhabit the second Heaven. The ancients could see evidence of the second Heaven in the night sky, naming constellations, marking the phases of the moon, and so forth.

We get a glimpse of the Bible's cosmology in Genesis, which informs us, "In the beginning, God created the heavens and the earth" (Gen. 1:1). The Hebrew word is *shamayim*, which means heights or elevations. The first two Heavens are above us, from an earthly perspective.

The third Heaven, however, is beyond us, which is why Yuri Gagarin could never see it. The third Heaven, you see, is the dwelling place of God, "who is the blessed and only Sovereign, the King of kings and Lord of lords, who alone has immortality, who dwells in unapproachable light, whom no one has ever seen or can see" (1 Tim. 6:15-16).

God dwells in "unapproachable light." So no one can see God in Heaven — the third Heaven — unless He allows it. Scripture, of course, gives us some intriguing pictures of what Heaven is like. Isaiah 6:1-3 says,

In the year that King Uzziah died I saw the Lord sitting upon a throne, high and lifted up; and the train of his robe filled the temple. Above him stood the seraphim. Each had six wings: with two he covered his face, and with two he covered his feet, and with two he flew. And one called to another and said:

"Holy, holy, holy is the LORD of hosts;
the whole earth is full of his glory!"

It is a powerful scene, and Isaiah is nearly undone, but for the grace
of God. It is very similar to what we saw in chapter 2, when the apostle
John was hurtled into the presence of God in Revelation 4. Let's revisit
this scene to pick up some fresh insights about Heaven. The language
and descriptions that John uses are fascinating.

First, he sees the Lord seated on His throne. "And he who sat there
had the appearance of jasper and carnelian," John reports in verse 3.
These two stones, interestingly, were the first and last stones on the
breastplate of the high priest, who served as a mediator, standing
between God and His people. In Revelation 21, the jasper stone is
described as being crystal clear, like a radiant diamond. The carnelian
stone is blood red, like a ruby. Notice that John says in verse 3 that the
Lord "had the appearance of." He is not saying he literally saw dia-
monds and rubies. He is saying it was like. In other words, John is
acknowledging that his first-century Greek is limited when it comes to
describing heavenly Reality. It was like. He is giving us an accurate,
though not exhaustive, glimpse of Heaven.

This struggling of John to put into words what he sees in the heavenly plane reminds me of Ezekiel's vision in Babylon among the exiles.

As I looked, behold, a stormy wind came out of the north, and a great
cloud, with brightness around it, and fire flashing forth continually,
and in the midst of the fire, *as it were* gleaming metal. And from the
midst of it came the *likeness* of four living creatures. And this was their
appearance: they had a human *likeness*, but each had four faces, and
each of them had four wings. Their legs were straight, and the soles of
their feet were *like* the sole of a calf's foot. And they sparkled *like* bur-
nished bronze. (Ezk. 1:4-7, emphases added)

Simile is piled on top of simile for Ezekiel. Try as he might, his
inspired words can only approximate what he sees of the heavenly

entourage by the Chebar canal. Words can only take us so far.

Second, John sees the twenty-four elders. In verse 4, the elders are wearing crowns. The Greek word, *stephanos*, means "that which surrounds." It is a victor's crown. We could compare this with winning the gold in the Olympics. In ancient Greek athletic competitions, the victor would receive a crown made of laurel leaves, a "perishable wreath" (1 Cor. 9:25). It is not a diadem, a crown of royalty, as worn by a king or a queen. It is a reward for faithfulness.

We find the *stephanos* elsewhere in Scripture. In Revelation 2:10, Jesus promises the church of Smyrna a crown of life because of their suffering. James 1:12 states that if we endure temptation, God will give us the crown of life. In 2 Timothy 4:8, Paul says that a crown of righteousness will be awarded to "all who have loved his appearing."

A friend of mine has run in a lot of triathlons. He has even competed in some Ironman events. He has a lot of ribbons and medals. One time I put about thirty of them around my neck. I looked like Mr. T on a bad day. I dared this guy to wear them publicly like that. Wisely, he refused.

Sometimes we imagine Heaven will be full of high achievers, those men and women whom God has blessed in an extraordinary way, walking around with three hundred medals or multiple crowns. Then they will look at our one little crown and say, "I have more crowns than you do." No. That is not the way it is. Heaven is not going to be full of boasting and selfish comparisons, thank God! Who could keep up?

Look at Revelation 4:10: "They cast their crowns before the throne." I love that. We don't win our crowns in order to boast. We'll never say, "Look at how much I have done." That's what we do, too often, here on earth. Heaven won't be like that. God will get all the glory. Yes, our labors will be recognized and are not ever going to be in vain (see 1 Cor. 15:58). But we did those tasks in His power, and only because He loved us first. All the glory will go to Him. When we see Him, we will gladly say, "Here, Lord, is my crown. Here, Lord, is my reward. Here, Lord, is my life. I give them back to You." What a relief! We don't have to carry the weight of our self-regard any more. We will be free!

What will our freedom look like in Heaven? I think we will have a perspective that is too often lacking here on earth. We will still be aware of things . . . but with perspective. We'll look at this issue in more depth in a later chapter.

It's true that in life we go through some very tough things. I've described some of my own to you in this volume. They are real, they are painful, and they are awful. There is no way to avoid them, as they are part and parcel of every human life. Yet while they seem to be the end of the world to us, with our limited perspective, they are not even close to that when we begin to see them from the vantage point of Heaven.

Think about Job for a moment. He loses his possessions, his children, and his health, for what reason he has no idea. All he is left with are his bitter and broken wife and his friends, who are "miserable comforters" (Job 16:2). Then he sees the greatness of God, and his calamities seem smaller somehow, even though he receives no divine explanation. Job has an inkling of Heaven (see 19:26), however, and he is willing to trust. When we get to Heaven, the circle will be completed, and we will finally know why. Remember, God sees our situation with perspective. Unlike us right now, God sees the big picture. The result, in His eyes, has already happened. It's going to be all right. Trust Him.

In Revelation 4, John is getting the divine perspective. Like Isaiah and Ezekiel, he sees some magnificent angelic creatures. Like them, he is awestruck. And like them, surely, he worships. Look at verse 10 again: "The twenty-four elders fall down before him who is seated on the throne and worship him who lives forever and ever."

One of the reasons we will engage in unbridled worship in Heaven is because we will know all things. All of our questions will be answered. All of our pain will be removed. All of our tears will be dried. At this point, worshiping will be like breathing.

Some people, however, fear that worshiping God for all eternity sounds kind of boring. For them, Heaven might be like a really long church service. That is not their idea of Heaven. They'd rather play golf or go bass fishing. Well, I don't know whether there will be golf or fishing in Heaven. If they are, praise God, and if they aren't, we won't miss them. So let me explain. First of all, let's be clear that worship, done in spirit and in truth, as Jesus says (see Jn. 4:23), is anything but boring. If you're bored in worship, believe me, the problem isn't with God.

What is the most amazing thing you have ever seen on this earth—a snow-capped mountain range, a new mother holding her baby, a beautiful sunset over the lapping waves as the day comes to a close? Whatever it is that really moves you, you want to share it, don't you? You want to tell others; you want them to see what you see, be touched by what touches you. You are excited by that special something, and it is the most natural thing in the world for you to praise it.

Friend, that is what worshiping in spirit and truth is all about. If you are excited by these good things on earth, just imagine how thrilling will be your worship of the Reality behind them in Heaven. No, heavenly worship will be anything but boring!

Yes, we will be joyfully worshiping the only Being in all the universe worthy of our worship. But we are going to do a lot more than that, besides. Revelation 7:15 says,

> They are before the throne of God,
>   and serve him day and night in his temple;
>   and he who sits on the throne will shelter them with his presence.

We will be serving God day and night. You might think that work is only for this world, a result of the Curse when Adam and Eve fell into sin. But the Lord gave our first parents work to do (see Gen. 1:28; 2:15) before they listened to the serpent and disobeyed Him (see 3:1-6). Work is not a punishment; it's part of our design as creatures made in the divine image. We will serve Him in the heavenly realms just as surely as we do in the earthly ones, only without sorrow and suffering. Work now can be fulfilling but also frustrating, purposeful and yet painful. Work then will be all sun and no shadow.

The same holds true with our giving. "If then you have not been faithful in the unrighteous wealth," Jesus said after another parable, "who will entrust to you the true riches?" (Lk. 16:11). Our faithful stewardship of our lives, resources, and abilities down here will have eternal consequences up there. That day is coming soon, perhaps more quickly than any of us expect. We will be in God's presence and will have to give an account. So what are we supposed to do in the interim?

I'll keep it simple. With apologies to Yuri Gagarin, this is not rocket science! Here is what you and I are to do. Like Enoch in the Old Testament, we are simply to walk with God. As Genesis 5:24 puts it so plainly and so beautifully, "Enoch walked with God, and he was not, for God took him." All we really have to do now is walk with God. Enoch walked with his Lord in the antediluvian world and made the transition to Heaven seamlessly. It was almost as if he was experiencing God in his day-to-day, earthly existence, until one day he stood before Him, face-to-face.

Walking connotes living your life. It speaks of effort. It speaks of regular motion. It speaks of consistency, day in and day out. It doesn't say Enoch sprinted with God, though sometimes God calls us to run the race (see Heb. 12:1). But Enoch walked with God, and we would do well to do the same. When we walk, we will see God. And the Bible commands us to walk:

- I say, walk by the Spirit, and you will not gratify the desires of the flesh. (Gal. 5:16)
- As you received Christ Jesus the Lord, so walk in him. (Col. 2:6)

Some Christians decide they are going to run for God. Sprint. All out. Full tilt. Then they collapse. So they get up again, sprint, and collapse again. And sprint and collapse. God would say to them, "How about just walking? Just be regular. Consistent. Every day. With Me."

Enoch walked with God.

Who sets the pace? God. Not me. The Lord says, "Let's slow down. I want to tell you something. Okay, now let's speed up a bit. Stay with Me." That is the idea. I am to stay in harmony with Him, neither running ahead nor lagging behind. I love Amos 3:3: "Do two walk together, unless they have agreed to meet?"

Some years ago, I went scuba diving in Hawaii. We did a rather deep dive of a hundred feet. We were led by a diving instructor who warned us to not use up all of the air in our tanks. I was so excited (and a bit stressed) by such a deep dive that I had almost emptied my tank by the time I had reached our depth. I gestured to the instructor that I was very low on air. He saw the somewhat panicked expression on my face through my fogged up mask and calmly gestured to the extra aqualung, known as the "octopus," attached to the back of his tank by a very short hose.

The octopus required me to hover barely above the instructor, so when he descended, so did I (with very shallow strokes). It was all a bit humiliating, but it sure beat the alternative . . . which was not breathing. That picture reminds me of what it means to stay in harmony with God. We go where He goes.

The Hebrew wording for together implies meeting at a fixed time and place.

Most of us respect other people enough to be on time for our appointments, don't we? If that's so, can you imagine being late for an appointment with the Creator, Sustainer, and Judge of the universe? Or skipping it altogether? I don't know what God might be calling you to do so that you can walk more consistently with Him. It might be to start (or end) the day with Him in prayer, to commit your life to Him, to think of Him, to focus on Him, to walk in harmony with Him. You want to be in tune with God so that, whether He comes tonight or a hundred years from now, it will be a seamless transition for you, as it was for Enoch.

One day, whenever it is, we will all have an appointment with God—an appointment when life on this earth will end and we will enter eternity. For believers, that will be a joyous time stepping into the third Heaven, as to be absent from the body is to be "at home with the Lord" (2 Cor. 5:8). You may think you know when that day will be, but trust me, you don't. No one does. So be ready. Walk with Him, starting right now. What we do now in this life provides a critical clue about where we will spend eternity. If you don't love Him now, in this life, you have no grounds for believing you will love Him in the next.

Remember, the ultimate goal is not to fly over Heaven, but to land there and to be welcomed as one of its citizens. But, how will we experience Heaven, and what will we know? Stay tuned!

CHAPTER 6

WHAT HEAVEN KNOWS
ABOUT EARTH

In the 1997 movie *Men in Black*, starring Will Smith and Tommy Lee Jones, space aliens are coming to earth about as often as a new "reality show" is created on television today. The powers-that-be fear that chaos will break out in human society if the existence of space aliens becomes known. So they create a secret agency that uses "neuralyzers" to erase and replace the memories of anyone who comes into contact with an extraterrestial.

Jones's character, Kay, works for the agency in charge of memory erasure, M.I.B. Kay has a new partner — Smith's character, named Jay. In one scene, a woman named Beatrice has just encountered an alien and must have her memory wiped clean. Kay uses the neuralyzer on her as Jay watches.

> **Kay:** All right, Beatrice, there was no alien. The flash of light you saw in the sky was not a UFO. Swamp gas from a weather balloon was trapped in a thermal pocket and reflected the light from Venus.
> **Jay:** Wait a minute. You just flash that thing, it erases her memory, and you just make up a new one?
> **Kay:** A standard issue neuralyzer.
> **Jay:** And that [stupid] story's the best you can come up with?[1]

Imagine for a minute what the world would be like if your memories could just be wiped clean. Author Rita Mae Brown once said, "One of the keys to happiness is a bad memory,"[2] and many of us would reflexively agree. But we would likely mean not that we would actually lose contact with an unhappy memory, but that we would choose not to dwell on it.

While certainly we probably wouldn't mind if some of our painful or embarrassing memories were neuralyzed—I certainly have a few potential candidates!—the fact is, most of us would probably rebel at having this kind of mental lobotomy. Losing our memories somehow is an attack on our dignity as humans, isn't it? That's one of the horrifying things about Alzheimer's and other brain diseases—the loss of memory and connection with our past.

So what does *Men in Black* have to do with Heaven and the afterlife? Well, I admit it—not a lot! But it illustrates in a small but significant way what many people think Heaven will be like. The idea of such folks is that nothing sad can ever touch our heavenly bliss. For them, this means that our bad memories, our pain, and our sadnesses will be wiped from our brains like a cloth going over a whiteboard. Some people say that once we are in Heaven, we will be so preoccupied with worshiping God that the last thing on our minds will be what is happening on earth. Besides, with all the tragedy and sadness in this world, they postulate, Heaven would just not be Heaven if we were still aware of these things.

To support this position, they might quote Revelation 21:4: "He will wipe away every tear from their eyes, and death shall be no more, neither shall there be mourning, nor crying, nor pain anymore, for the former things have passed away." According to this theory, if God is going to wipe away our tears, He will first have to wipe away our memories, or at least the bad ones.

This understanding seems similar to a nineteenth century misunderstanding about Heaven. Back in the early days of the American experiment, the Puritans wrote extensively about what awaits believers in Heaven. They were a God-focused bunch who sought to exalt our Creator, in Heaven and on earth. One of the best Puritan writers on the topic was Richard Baxter, who said with anticipation that we will be employed in singing God's praises for all eternity.

> As God will have from them a spiritual worship, suited to his own spiritual being, he will provide them a spiritual rest, suitable to their spiritual nature. The knowledge of God and his Christ, a delightful complacency in that mutual love, an everlasting rejoicing in the enjoyment of our God, with a perpetual singing of his high praises; this is Heaven for a saint.[3]

It's a beautiful, if incomplete, picture of Heaven. However, some others who came later, steeped in the activist, can-do spirit of the frontier, found this vision of Heaven "unattractive, even repellent."[4] One was author Elizabeth Stuart Phelps, whose character Mary Cabot found the Puritan ideal of Heaven full of "glittering generalities, cold commonplace, vagueness, unreality, a God and a future at which I sat and shivered." Contemplating a heavenly worship scene from Revelation, Mary is disturbed.

> There was something about adoration, and the harpers harping with their harps, and the sea of glass, and crying "Worthy the Lamb!" And a great deal more than that bewildered and disheartened me so that I could scarcely listen to it. I do not doubt that we shall glorify God primarily and happily, but can we not do it in some other way than by harping and praying?[5]

Joni Eareckson Tada recounts a conversation about Heaven she had with a Christian friend not long after the diving accident that left her a quadriplegic. Her friend, Steve Estes, was trying to get this wheelchair-bound young woman excited about Heaven. So he turned to the New Testament's descriptions. There would be a new Heaven and a new earth, he said. What Joni heard, however, was not all that she would be getting, but all she would be losing, in Heaven. After all, "the former things have passed away."

No more sea. No more night. No more time. No more moon or sun. And what about food, marriage, sex, art, and great books? . . . Sitting in a wheelchair for decades has loaded me with a lifetime of glorious memories, everything from feeling my fingers on the cool ivory keys of a piano to the euphoria of diving through the breakers at high tide. Such memories flood every nerve and fiber of my being and, thus, my imagination. It's awful to think that the best stuff of which memories are made will have no place in Heaven.[6]

Thank God, Joni no longer has that view of Heaven as a place of negation, where all good is removed, where we are forever disconnected from the world, from our memories, and from knowledge about those who loved us. In this view, we are so busy worshiping that we are unaware of the passing of time, if there even is such a thing as time in Heaven.

Worshiping forever may sound appealing to some and, frankly, really scary to others. To some ears, it sounds like a really long church service—a really boring church service—the kind during which you're always checking your watch or smartphone, thinking about lunch, or daydreaming about the game on TV.

We've all been to services that went just a little bit too long and found ourselves getting turned off. Hey, I've preached at some of those services and was bored listening to myself! It happens, but sometimes we worry whether Heaven will be just like one of those interminable church services—but without the prospect of lunch or a good game. Maybe we don't particularly like the music, the pews, or the people. Maybe the color of the church carpet annoys us.

If that's what you think Heaven will be like, then please listen closely. Heaven is not going to be a long, boring church service. Yes, as we have seen, there will be worship, and plenty of it—but it will be the kind of worship that you will never want to stop doing. Yet we can worship God in more ways than simply attending a church service. As we saw in 1 Corinthians 10:31, "Whether you eat or drink, or whatever you do, do all to the glory of God." We can worship God any number of ways here on earth — and not just on Sunday morning. We can even eat and drink as acts of worship.

Do we somehow think that we will have fewer opportunities to worshipfully serve and enjoy Him in Heaven? Perish the thought! Our fear of boredom in Heaven reflects a lack of holy imagination on our part, not a lack of excitement on Heaven's part. We will be fully engaged in heavenly worship, and, even more thrilling, we will have an eye on earth as well. That perception will help us appreciate God's grace in eternally meaningful ways.

So if our memories are not wiped clean in Heaven, what do people in Heaven know about what is going on here on earth? Do they care about us? Are they perhaps watching us right now? Some people here on earth think that folks up in Heaven are just sitting there watching our every move — as if we are almost their form of entertainment. "Well, John, what are we going to do today up on this cloud? Let's turn on the television and watch what's happening down on earth" — you know, as in *It's a Wonderful Life*.

Others might think that sometimes people in Heaven will come down and intervene in our lives, as in *Highway to Heaven*, directing our steps and helping us know what to do. So which view is correct? Are people blissfully unaware in Heaven, or do they have ringside seats for the nightly earthly boxing matches? Actually, I believe that both views are incorrect in their own way.

People in Heaven definitely have some knowledge about what is happening here on earth. Let me take it a step further. I think people in Heaven know a lot more about earth than we may realize. In Heaven, we will be in our glorified state. We won't know less in Heaven than we know on earth. We'll know more. But we also need to realize that people in Hell also have some awareness of at least some earthly events, too. Let's deal with Heaven first, by observing the following scene.

> When he opened the fifth seal, I saw under the altar the souls of those who had been slain for the word of God and for the witness they had borne. They cried out with a loud voice, "O Sovereign Lord, holy and

true, how long before you will judge and avenge our blood on those who dwell on the earth?" Then they were each given a white robe and told to rest a little longer, until the number of their fellow servants and their brothers should be complete, who were to be killed as they themselves had been. (Rev. 6:9-11)

Notice here that these are martyrs who have gone to Heaven. See how they are aware of what is happening on the earth. For instance, they know they were killed for following Christ. Thus, there is a direct continuity between our identity on earth and our identity in Heaven. We are not different people when we get to Heaven. We are the same people . . . relocated and glorified.

These martyrs are fully conscious, rational, and aware of each other, of God, and of the situation on earth. They remember that they were killed for their faith in Jesus. People who say that we don't remember anything about earth need to grapple with what these martyrs know. They remember. These are not angels. They are people who have died and gone to the other side.

In addition, they are aware of the passing of time on earth. In Revelation 6:10, they ask, "How long before you will judge and avenge our blood on those who dwell on the earth?" "How long?" they ask.

I spoke earlier in this book about the heavenly perspective we will have when we go to Heaven, and these martyrs certainly have it. They possess a clear sense of justice. We will talk more about this later, but clearly they want those who murdered them for their faith to get what is coming to them. They desire God's justice to be done on earth as it is in Heaven. Suffice it to say here that there is a continuity in their perceptions of life on earth and in Heaven.

Now let's turn to another heavenly scene, based in Luke 16, the story[7] that Jesus told about a rich man and a poor man. One went to a place of comfort referred to (in the King James Version) as "Abraham's bosom." Apparently they were reclining together at the banquet table, in the ancient way. The other went to a place of torment described as Hades. Here is Jesus' account of what happened.

There was a rich man who was clothed in purple and fine linen and who feasted sumptuously every day. And at his gate was laid a poor man named Lazarus, covered with sores, who desired to be fed with what fell from the rich man's table. Moreover, even the dogs came and licked his sores. The poor man died and was carried by the angels to Abraham's side. The rich man also died and was buried, and in Hades, being in torment, he lifted up his eyes and saw Abraham far off and Lazarus at his side. And he called out, "Father Abraham, have mercy on me, and send Lazarus to dip the end of his finger in water and cool my tongue, for I am in anguish in this flame." But Abraham said, "Child, remember that you in your lifetime received your good things, and Lazarus in like manner bad things; but now he is comforted here, and you are in anguish. And besides all this, between us and you a great chasm has been fixed, in order that those who would pass from here to you may not be able, and none may cross from there to us." And he said, "Then I beg you, father, to send him to my father's house — for I have five brothers — so that he may warn them, lest they also come into this place of torment." But Abraham said, "They have Moses and the Prophets; let them hear them." And he said, "No, father Abraham, but if someone goes to them from the dead, they will repent." He said to him, "If they do not hear Moses and the Prophets, neither will they be convinced if someone should rise from the dead." (Lk. 16:19-31)

You might wonder how this picture of the afterlife, in which the saved and the damned can see one another, fits in with other biblical accounts, where there is no sign of the lost in Heaven. The short answer is that the architecture of the afterlife, if you will, changed with the death and resurrection of Jesus. Before that epochal event, when believers died, they went to Abraham's bosom, awaiting the time when Christ would die and open the door of Heaven. Hades was also a place of waiting but, as this passage shows, also a place of torment.

One of the men is identified as Lazarus. He lived off the scraps that fell from the table of the "rich man." Yet death knocked at both doors. Death is no respecter of persons. It doesn't matter if you are wealthy or impoverished, famous or unknown. Everyone dies. Death is the great equalizer. On the other side, however, not everything is equal. In fact, the rich man is in torment, and the poor man, Lazarus, is in Abraham's bosom.

And please take note of this fact: Both men are fully conscious on the other side. Although they are kept from going to each other because of the "great chasm" between them, they are aware of one another's existence. The rich man sees Lazarus from a distance and even uses his name. He is aware of their prior history, of which Abraham reminds him: "Child, remember that you in your lifetime received your good things, and Lazarus in like manner bad things; but now he is comforted here, and you are in anguish."

The rich man remembers his life on earth even while he is in torment, making his suffering all the more bitter. While we receive no word from Lazarus in this scene, it seems probable, because he is with Abraham, that he hears and understands the entire conversation. He remembers his former poverty, making his comfort with Abraham all the sweeter.

We see a similar dynamic in an Old Testament account of Saul and Samuel. In disguise, Saul, facing a desperate battle against the Philistines, calls up the deceased prophet Samuel through a medium at En-dor.

The woman said, "Whom shall I bring up for you?" He said, "Bring up Samuel for me." When the woman saw Samuel, she cried out with a loud voice. And the woman said to Saul, "Why have you deceived me? You are Saul." The king said to her, "Do not be afraid. What do you see?" And the woman said to Saul, "I see a god coming up out of the earth." He said to her, "What is his appearance?" And she said, "An old man is coming up, and he is wrapped in a robe." And Saul knew that it was Samuel, and he bowed with his face to the ground and paid homage.

Then Samuel said to Saul, "Why have you disturbed me by

bringing me up?" Saul answered, "I am in great distress, for the Philistines are warring against me, and God has turned away from me and answers me no more, either by prophets or by dreams. Therefore I have summoned you to tell me what I shall do." And Samuel said, "Why then do you ask me, since the LORD has turned from you and become your enemy? The LORD has done to you as he spoke by me, for the LORD has torn the kingdom out of your hand and given it to your neighbor, David. Because you did not obey the voice of the LORD and did not carry out his fierce wrath against Amalek, therefore the LORD has done this thing to you this day. Moreover, the LORD will give Israel also with you into the hand of the Philistines, and tomorrow you and your sons shall be with me. The LORD will give the army of Israel also into the hand of the Philistines."

Then Saul fell at once full length on the ground, filled with fear because of the words of Samuel. (1 Sam. 28:11-20)

Samuel, from the other side, recognizes Saul and remembers their mutual history. He also remembers God working through him while he lived on the earth. Through God, he even predicts Saul's coming death—accurately. For his part, Saul is enabled to recognize Samuel, and he is seized with dread. While some of the details in this account are a bit murky, it seems clear that those on the other side are aware of life back on earth, at least to a certain extent.

Back in Luke 16, what else does the rich man, known as Dives in church tradition, know? Well, the rich man in torment knows that his five brothers are lost. He says, "I beg you, father, to send him to my father's house—for I have five brothers—so that he may warn them, lest they also come into this place of torment." "Dives" does not want them to end up on the wrong side of the chasm. Clearly, people in eternity are aware of the fact that loved ones are not saved. This indicates knowledge in eternity about what is happening on earth.

In the afterlife, we are the same people, with real memories of what went on in our lives on earth. You will know more in Heaven than you know on earth, not less. We don't all get a collective lobotomy when we go to glory. There is no heavenly neuralyzer. You will remember things. If you did not remember anything in the afterlife, then why would God open the books to judge you according to your works (see Rev. 20:12)? He wants you to see how your life on earth has determined your eternal destiny. You will see clearly, probably more clearly than you ever have before.

So we need to make sure that we are ready to meet the Lord. In the story of the rich man and the poor man, remember that one of them went to torment. The other went to comfort. Their destinations were decided by what happened *on earth*. What we do on earth has repercussions in eternity.

This is of eternal import, so listen as if your life depended on it — because it does: You decide where you will go. You decide if you will go to Heaven. You decide if you will go to Hell. God doesn't want you to go to Hell. He says, "For I have no pleasure in the death of anyone, declares the Lord God; so turn, and live" (Ezk. 18:32). He wants you to join Him in Heaven. But you must respond to His offer of forgiveness. At the cross, Christ died in our place. At the tomb, He rose again from the dead. If we will but turn from our sin and put our faith in Jesus, we can know with confidence that we will go to Heaven when we die.

> While we were still weak, at the right time Christ died for the ungodly. For one will scarcely die for a righteous person — though perhaps for a good person one would dare even to die — but God shows his love for us in that while we were still sinners, Christ died for us. Since, therefore, we have now been justified by his blood, much more shall we be saved by him from the wrath of God. For if while we were enemies we were reconciled to God by the death of his Son, much more, now that we are reconciled, shall we be saved by his life. (Ro. 5:6-10)

Are you ready? Are you sure? Do you know with confidence that you would go to Heaven if you died today? Do you know with certainty that if Christ were to come back again that you would be ready to meet Him? And what about your friends and family? Don't wait until it is too late to tell them, as the rich man did, to his eternal sorrow. "Behold," God says, "now is the favorable time; behold, now is the day of salvation" (2 Cor. 6:2). Don't wait. Do it now.

America is a culture that avoids the subject of death at all costs. Instead, we focus on increasing the quantity *and* quality of our limited days on this planet. Not an hour goes by that we are not warned about this cancer, or that infection. We are told to diet, exercise, put on our seatbelts, avoid texting while driving, eat more fish and less fat, get regular checkups, and so on. Each of these bits of advice has its place, but taken as a whole, these avoidance strategies betray a certain fear of death. And when someone we personally know or know about does die, we will avoid that dreaded "D-word" and instead say, "He passed on." Or we may choose to be more flippant, saying, "She kicked the bucket," or, "He cashed in his chips."

This is because we don't want to deal with the reality of something as permanent and seemingly unknowable as death. We are happy to celebrate an earthly life of accomplishment while never asking the obvious question, "Where does this person go now?"

When Jesus was crucified, the man on the cross next to Him wanted to know. So he asked the Lord for mercy, and Jesus said to him, "Truly, I say to you, *today* you will be with me in Paradise" (Lk. 23:43, emphasis added). That very day, the thief who had been crucified next to Jesus went into a place of waiting, a realm of bliss and comfort called Paradise. This was three days before Jesus had been raised from the dead. But the Bible says that after the Lord's death and resurrection, a believer who dies goes straight to Heaven and into the presence of God. As the apostle Paul said, to be absent from the body is to be present with the Lord (see 2 Cor. 5:8).

You might describe what happened to this thief as a deathbed conversion. I hope this fact gives a measure of encouragement for you to never stop praying for friends and loved ones who are still outside of Jesus Christ. Time and again, I've heard stories of people who have come to the Lord right before passing into eternity.

Sometimes we think of someone who has died and fear he or she is in Hell right now. I've actually heard people say, "That person is in Hell." The truth is, you and I don't know who is in Hell. We're in no position to say. Now I *do* think we can authoritatively say if someone is in *Heaven*.

If that person has put his or her faith in Christ, we can say, "This person is with the Lord now." But who are we to say what may or may not have happened to an individual in those final seconds before leaving this life and entering the next?

I know this: If people cry out to Jesus in repentance with their last breaths or final, fading thoughts, God will forgive them and accept them into Heaven. He did it for the thief, after all.

And as we and our loved ones experience His salvation in Heaven, we will gain a whole new level of clarity on what our gracious God is really like. It is to that subject that we turn in our next chapter.

CHAPTER 7

WHEN SEEING IS BELIEVING

I love the apostle John, and so did Jesus. Over and over, John referred to himself in the third person as "the disciple whom Jesus loved" (see Jn. 13:23; 20:2; and so on). Here are some indications of the love Jesus had for John, and why:

- John was part of that inner group of three men who often accompanied the Lord on special missions — with Peter and James (see, for example, Mk. 5:37).
- John was there when Jesus was transfigured with Moses and Elijah and His clothing shined like the sun (see Mt. 17:1).
- John was there in the Garden of Gethsemane, where Jesus prayed, "My Father, if it is possible, let this cup pass from Me; yet not as I will, but as You will" (Mt. 26:39, NASB).
- John went with Peter to the courtyard of the high priest but never denied his Lord, as Peter did (see Jn. 18:15-16).
- To his eternal credit, among the men who followed Jesus, John — and John alone — stood at the foot of the cross after our Lord had been crucified (see Jn. 19:26-27). When the others were in hiding, there stood John. Maybe that is one of the reasons Christ gave John the mission of caring for His mother: "Behold, your mother," He said, referring to Mary. John adds, "And from that hour the disciple took her to his own home" (19:27).

- When John and Peter ran together to the empty tomb (see John 20), John got there first, most likely because he was faster. John looked in and saw the tomb was empty. He also saw the bandages wrapped in sort of a mummy-like shape around where the body of Christ had been. Peter saw this and wondered what it was all about. But John, we are told, "saw and believed" (20:8).

John seemed to be a little more perceptive spiritually than the other disciples. Maybe that is because he was always so close to the Lord. At the Last Supper, we read of John leaning his head on the chest of Jesus so he would not miss a single word (see John 13). Talk about spiritual intimacy! After Christ was risen again from the dead, He called to the disciples on the shore of Galilee. It was John, before anybody else, who said, "It is the Lord" (21:7). John was a very insightful person.

Though he is an eyewitness to the Resurrection, John is a firm believer in the need to exercise faith, what Hebrews 11:1 calls "the assurance of things hoped for, the conviction of things not seen." A key scene for the apostle occurs when the resurrected Jesus appears to Thomas, who has doubted earlier reports from the apostles and other believers that the Lord has been raised.

Thomas, one of the Twelve, called the Twin, was not with them when Jesus came. So the other disciples told him, "We have seen the Lord." But he said to them, "Unless I see in his hands the mark of the nails, and place my finger into the mark of the nails, and place my hand into his side, I will never believe."

Eight days later, his disciples were inside again, and Thomas was with them. Although the doors were locked, Jesus came and stood among them and said, "Peace be with you." Then he said to Thomas, "Put your finger here, and see my hands; and put out your hand, and place it in my side. Do not disbelieve, but believe." Thomas answered him, "My Lord and my God!" Jesus said to him, "Have you believed because you have seen me? Blessed are those who have not seen and yet have believed." (Jn. 20:24-29)

This statement is not surprising. Jesus valued faith over sight when He came the first time. According to the prophet Isaiah, the Lord generally went around unannounced by Heaven and unrecognized by men, at least at first.

Who has believed what he has heard from us?
    And to whom has the arm of the Lord been revealed?
For he grew up before him like a young plant,
    and like a root out of dry ground;
he had no form or majesty that we should look at him,
    and no beauty that we should desire him.
He was despised and rejected by men;
    a man of sorrows, and acquainted with grief;
and as one from whom men hide their faces
    he was despised, and we esteemed him not. (Is. 53:1-3)

Why was Jesus' identity so often hidden behind His humility? Why didn't He just make it plain? Why not simply burst into the world with miraculous power and finish the job? C. S. Lewis thought that God is waiting now so that people can exercise faith now — before it is too late.

He wants to give us the chance of joining His side freely. I do not suppose you and I would have thought much of a Frenchman who waited till the Allies were marching into Germany and then announced he was on our side. God will invade. But I wonder whether people who ask God to interfere openly and directly in our world quite realize what it will be like when He does. When that happens, it is the end of the world. When the author walks on to the stage the play is over. God is going to invade, all right: but what is the good of saying you are on His side then, when you see the whole natural universe melting away like a dream and something else — something it never entered your head to conceive — comes crashing in; something so beautiful to some of us and so terrifying to others that none of us will have any choice left?[1]

So Jesus' glory was shrouded most days. Certainly Jesus Himself left enough clues so that people with genuine spiritual interest and faith could believe in Him. His dialogue with the woman at the well (see John 4), His miraculous encounter with fisherman Peter (see Lk. 6:1-11), and His knowledge of Nathanael's character (see Jn. 1:47-51) brought people gently to a recognition of His divinity.

Occasionally, however, Jesus left stronger hints. We have several fascinating accounts of the shrouds of Heaven, as it were, being pulled back, with just a few celestial glimmers peeking through into our world. The Transfiguration, which I mentioned above, is one such incident.

> Six days later Jesus took with Him Peter and James and John his brother, and led them up on a high mountain by themselves. And He was transfigured before them; and His face shone like the sun, and His garments became as white as light. And behold, Moses and Elijah appeared to them, talking with Him. Peter said to Jesus, "Lord, it is good for us to be here; if You wish, I will make three tabernacles here, one for You, and one for Moses, and one for Elijah." While he was still speaking, a bright cloud overshadowed them, and behold, a voice out of the cloud said, "This is My beloved Son, with whom I am well-pleased; listen to Him!" When the disciples heard *this*, they fell face down to the ground and were terrified. And Jesus came to *them* and touched them and said, "Get up, and do not be afraid." And lifting up their eyes, they saw no one except Jesus Himself alone. (Mt. 17:1-8, NASB)

The real miracle is not that Jesus shined like the sun before His disciples. No, the real miracle is that He did not shine all the time! He never lost His glory. He only shrouded it as He walked our earth, breathed our air, felt our pain, and ultimately died our death.

A similar heavenly bursting forth occurred when Jesus was born in Bethlehem: "And suddenly there was with the angel a multitude of the heavenly host praising God and saying, 'Glory to God in the highest, and on earth peace among those with whom he is pleased!'" (Lk. 2:13-14).

Then there is the account of what happened when Jesus was baptized by another John—the Baptist:

> In those days Jesus came from Nazareth of Galilee and was baptized by John in the Jordan. And when he came up out of the water, immediately he saw the heavens being torn open and the Spirit descending on him like a dove. And a voice came from heaven, "You are my beloved Son; with you I am well pleased." (Mk. 1:9-11)

Even the rocks on occasion threatened to burst forth with the news of Jesus' identity (see Lk. 19:40).

But despite all this evidence, the climactic moment for John is when Jesus tells Thomas, "Blessed are those who have not seen and yet have believed." Most of the time, John seems to be saying, we must believe without seeing. Faith is indeed the assurance of things not seen (see Heb. 11:1).

But now John is near the end of his life, and he is privileged to see the Lord for perhaps one last time. The old apostle is on the island of Patmos. I don't want you to think he is enjoying some beautiful little paradise, hanging out, catching rays, surfing, having a great old time. No. This is a lonely island in the Aegean—only 13 square miles, cold, windy, with little vegetation. It's not much more than a rock in the ocean—not a pleasant place to be.

The Romans have sent John here because, according to church tradition, they put him in a pot of boiling oil but he wouldn't cook. They thought, "Well, he is an old man. He doesn't have long to live. Let's just banish him." So they have sent him off to Patmos, never expecting to hear from him again.

The church of which John is a leader is under intense persecution. All of the other apostles have died or been murdered for their faith at this point. The persecution started under Nero and continued through other Roman emperors, such as Diocletian. Many believers are still losing their lives. Uncertainty about the future is pervasive. Families are being torn apart. Christians are being arrested and put to death—some of them tortured first.

Yet John has the last word over the powers that be. On this supposedly God-forsaken island, God gives him the book of Revelation. Not only this, but God gives John a picture of the Lord that will sustain him—and us—through any doubts, any trials, any hardships. He shows John a time and a place when seeing will be believing and faith will be sight.

> The revelation of Jesus Christ, which God gave him to show to his servants the things that must soon take place. He made it known by sending his angel to his servant John, who bore witness to the word of God and to the testimony of Jesus Christ, even to all that he saw. Blessed is the one who reads aloud the words of this prophecy, and blessed are those who hear, and who keep what is written in it, for the time is near. (Rev. 1:1-3)

This revelation is from Jesus Christ. The Greek word for "revelation" is *apocalypsis*. From this word we get Apocalypse, another title for the book of Revelation. In this book, Jesus Christ is in Heaven revealing Himself to us, as truly He is when the heavenly shroud is torn away. This revelation is "from Jesus Christ the faithful witness, the firstborn of the dead, and the ruler of kings on earth" (1:5).

What does John mean when he says Jesus is "the faithful witness"? At a minimum it means that Jesus is telling the truth about Himself. While many people today have an *opinion* about Jesus—the Son of God, a religious leader, a revolutionary, a misunderstood prophet—we ought to listen to what Jesus says about Himself. After all, who is a better source on you than you? Who is a better source on Jesus than Jesus?

Jesus knows His story better than anyone. One Sunday, the risen Lord walked incognito with two confused and despondent disciples on the Emmaus Road:

> That very day two of them were going to a village named Emmaus, about seven miles from Jerusalem, and they were talking with each other about all these things that had happened. While they were talking and discussing together, Jesus himself drew near and went with them. But their eyes were kept from recognizing him. And he said to them, "What is this conversation that you are holding with each other as you walk?" And they stood still, looking sad. Then one of them, named Cleopas, answered him, "Are you the only visitor to Jerusalem who does not know the things that have happened there in these days?" And he said to them, "What things?" And they said to him, "Concerning Jesus of Nazareth, a man who was a prophet mighty in deed and word before God and all the people, and how our chief priests and rulers delivered him up to be condemned to death, and crucified him. But we had hoped that he was the one to redeem Israel. Yes, and besides all this, it is now the third day since these things happened. Moreover, some women of our company amazed us. They were at the tomb early in the morning, and when they did not find his body, they came back saying that they had even seen a vision of angels, who said that he was alive. Some of those who were with us went to the tomb and found it just as the women had said, but him they did not see." And he said to them, "O foolish ones, and slow of heart to believe all that the prophets have spoken! Was it not necessary that the Christ should suffer these things and enter into his glory?" And beginning with Moses and all the Prophets, he interpreted to them in all the Scriptures the things concerning himself. (Lk. 24:13-27)

These disciples understood the *fact* of the Crucifixion, but they had failed utterly to grasp its *meaning*. So Jesus took it upon Himself to tell them all about Jesus. He pointed out all of the Scriptures that alluded to the fact that He was going to suffer and die. He could do this because He is an expert on Himself. He is a *faithful* witness.

Not every witness is faithful, of course. We all know people who sometimes stretch the truth. They do it to look good, to feel better about themselves, or to gain a particular advantage that telling the unvarnished truth would not afford them. We tell lies because we don't like or agree with the reality of our experience. "Lies are like wishes," says Bella DePaulo, a social psychologist who studies deception for the University of Virginia. "Behind almost every lie there is a wish that the lie was true."[2]

Sometimes people lie outright, of course, and this undermines social cohesion. Even in a court of law, where people are *sworn* to tell the truth, witnesses will sometimes tell untruths. Attorneys will press these witnesses for any inconsistencies in their stories. If they are caught lying, they are liable to be charged with perjury, which is a serious offense. Truth is a prerequisite to the law, to business, to good personal relationships, to scientific advancement, and to psychological health. So even though many people lie to enhance their own personal agendas, they will acknowledge the need for everyone *else* to tell the truth. George Orwell knew how easy it is for people to deceive themselves.

"The point is that we are all capable of believing things which we know to be untrue, and then, when we are finally proved wrong, impudently twisting the facts so as to show that we were right," Orwell wrote in his 1946 essay "In Front of Your Nose." He continued: "Intellectually, it is possible to carry on this process for an indefinite time: the only check on it is that sooner or later a false belief bumps up against solid reality, usually on a battlefield."[3]

So if being a faithful witness is important on earth, imagine how much more important it is in Heaven. According to Revelation 1, Jesus is a faithful witness. Not only that, He is *the* faithful witness. He truly is the only One who always lives in a "no spin zone." Jesus is "the truth" (Jn. 14:6). As such, He gives us "the truth, the whole truth, and nothing but the truth," on earth as it is in Heaven.

But not only does He tell us the truth. He gives it to us lovingly. Here is the rest of Revelation 1:5: "To him who loves us and has freed us from our sins by his blood."

Jesus loves us more than anyone else. So when He speaks faithfully, we can be assured He is also speaking lovingly. Everyone knows that you can be truthful and not loving. There are a lot of things that are true that one should not necessarily say out loud. Sometimes we say that someone is "brutally honest," because the truth can hurt . . . deeply. We may think unkind thoughts about others, and they may even be true (though not always). But we usually don't *say* them, because to speak them aloud would be hurtful and embarrassing.

There is a reason the apostle Paul tells us to speak the truth in love (see Eph. 4:15), because sometimes we are tempted to be "brutally honest." No one ever has to remind Jesus to speak the truth in love, because He is ever the faithful and loving witness.

Look at Revelation 1:5 again. A better translation would be "He *keeps on* loving us." Although we know salvation is solely by God's grace and we don't deserve it, sometimes we begin to think that we must do certain things to merit the continuing love of God. We do this because that's sometimes how it is with our fellow human beings, or even with us. We attach strings to our love. We say (or at least think), "If you do this, then I will love you. If you don't, then I won't." Friend, that is a recipe for insecurity, on earth and in Heaven. But Jesus isn't like that. The love of God is consistent. It is persistent. He says, "Yea, I have loved thee with an everlasting love: therefore with lovingkindness have I drawn thee" (Jer. 31:3, KJV).

What a contrast is the love of God with the so-called love of our culture or our world. God's love is unconditional and permanent. The world's love is conditional and temporary. Our heavenly Father says, "For I the LORD do not change; therefore you, O children of Jacob, are not consumed" (Mal. 3:6). Our earthly taskmasters ask, "What have you done for me lately?"

Our world loves you when you are young and beautiful. God loves you when you are old and ugly (or smelly). Our world loves you when you are famous. God loves you when you are unknown. I think of my aunt, Willie Jordan, who has worked tirelessly on the streets of skid row in Los Angeles for almost all of her life. She has distributed food and clothing to thousands of people who had lost hope. She founded a mission more than sixty years ago with my Uncle Fred called "The Fred Jordan Mission." She is intent on bringing the values of Heaven to bear on the callousness of earth. Our world loves the rich and powerful. God loves the poor and weak. Our world loves the extraordinary. God loves the ordinary—people like you and me.

Take a final look at Revelation 1:5. God has demonstrated this love for us in a tangible way. Jesus showed supreme love by dying for us: The Lord "has freed us from our sins by his blood." I want you to notice the tense of the verb. Jesus has freed you from your sins if you trust in Him. God has forgiven you through Christ for all of the wrong you have ever done. Jesus said, "Greater love has no one than this, that someone lay down his life for his friends" (Jn. 15:13).

This persistent, unconditional, self-giving love of God lays the groundwork for what John sees in Revelation 1:7:

> Behold, he is coming with the clouds, and every eye will see him, even those who pierced him, and all tribes of the earth will wail on account of him. Even so. Amen.

Friend, the Author is going to come down from Heaven and step onto the world stage one last time. As the angels told the disciples right after Jesus ascended into Heaven,

> Men of Galilee, why do you stand looking into heaven? This Jesus, who was taken up from you into heaven, will come in the same way as you saw him go into heaven. (Acts 1:11)

Yes, Jesus, who came incognito the first time, will come in unmistakable power and great glory the final time. He will come as He went—visibly, bodily, and miraculously. We will examine the Lord's Second Advent in a subsequent chapter, but suffice it to say right now that this will be a clarifying moment for all of us. We will finally know with absolute certainty where we stand with the Lord. All doubt will be removed — about Him, and about ourselves. And John tells us that this will not be a happy realization for many, who will "wail."

Today, of course, everyone has an idea about Jesus, and in our tolerant age, every opinion is given equal weight. Muslims believe He was a prophet but not the Son of God. Hindus are happy to give Jesus some space alongside the other figurines on their god shelf. New atheists decry the supposedly poisonous properties of the religion founded in His name. Some religion scholars believe that Jesus was a nice man who was badly misunderstood and wound up dying for it. Others, including me, believe Jesus is the Truth, the eternal Son of God, the second person of the Trinity, who came down from Heaven to free us from our sins by dying on the cross and then rising from the dead.

Though there is good historical, theological, and sociological evidence to believe that Jesus is who He said He is (and we have looked at some of it in this book), the fact is, there will always be disputes in the realm where faith is the assurance of things unseen, where those who do *not* see are the ones who are blessed. But the first chapter of Revelation reminds us that a day is coming, perhaps very soon, when seeing will be believing.

John, at a point in his life when discouragement would have been easy, gets a heavenly preview of who Jesus is, with the shroud of Heaven torn away.

> Then I turned to see the voice that was speaking to me, and on turning I saw seven golden lampstands, and in the midst of the lampstands one like a son of man, clothed with a long robe and with a golden sash around his chest. The hairs of his head were white, like white wool, like snow. His eyes were like a flame of fire, his feet were like burnished bronze, refined in a furnace, and his voice was like the roar of many waters. In his right hand he held seven stars, from his mouth came a sharp two-edged sword, and his face was like the sun shining in full strength. (Rev. 1:12-16)

In Heaven, there will be no doubt about who is in charge of the universe. In Heaven, there will be no debate about who Christ is. In Heaven, the saints will see Him in all His glory. In Heaven, there will no longer be any speculation about who or what is "true." Remember this the next time you are tempted to doubt or to be discouraged.

Faith is a virtue on earth, not in Heaven. Why? Because we won't need it there! Faith is the bridge between Heaven and earth. Once we have crossed it, we will never need it again. So in the meantime, hold onto your faith like a little child. Hang in there, no matter what this world throws at you, no matter what island they banish you. Clarity is coming. As the apostle Paul said, "For now we see in a mirror dimly, but then face to face. Now I know in part; then I shall know fully, even as I have been fully known" (1 Cor. 13:12).

Seeing God face-to-face will be a wonderful heavenly Reality for believers. Yet there are some beings who already have that privilege—angels, who, Jesus said, "always see the face of my Father who is in heaven" (Mt. 18:10). What can we learn about Heaven from these celestial beings that will influence our life here on earth? Stay tuned.

HEAVEN'S MESSENGERS

According to most physicists today, the matter that we can see with our eyes and measure with our instruments constitutes only a small fraction of the universe. The rest they call "dark matter."[1] Though we can't perceive its presence with our five senses, dark matter apparently exerts a powerful, if unseen influence, over the cosmos. It took scientists a long time to acknowledge the real but hidden existence of dark matter, because it seems so counterintuitive to our everyday experience.

Christians, however, shouldn't be surprised when asked to believe in unseen realities in our physical universe, because we know about so many unseen realities in the heavenlies. As we discussed in the previous chapter, faith itself is the assurance of things *unseen*. We often don't see heavenly realities except out of the corner of our eye, when we are not looking for them. God asks us to take a lot of things on faith in the present age, because so much must remain hidden for the time being. This is especially true when it comes to unseen spiritual realities. Yet they are, like dark matter, just as real as you and me.

The book of Second Kings gives us a glimpse into these unseen realities in an illuminating account of the prophet Elisha and his servant, Gehazi. One morning, Gehazi got up and saw to his horror that the whole town was ringed with enemy soldiers. In a panic, Gehazi ran to wake up his master.

"What are we going to do?" he wailed.

We can imagine Elisha sitting up in bed and wiping the sleep out of his eyes, trying to digest this news. Apparently, it didn't take him long, because we read these words:

> He said, "Do not be afraid, for those who are with us are more than those who are with them." Then Elisha prayed and said, "O Lᴏʀᴅ, please open his eyes that he may see." So the Lᴏʀᴅ opened the eyes of the young man, and he saw, and behold, the mountain was full of horses and chariots of fire all around Elisha. (2 K. 6:16-17)

"Open his eyes." If our spiritual eyes could only be opened for a moment or two, we, too, would see the angelic forces of God, surrounding us and protecting us. Right along with Elisha we have the privilege of saying, "Those who are with us are more than those who are with them."

Actually, lots of us already believe in angels. *Time* magazine reported on a study that found a whopping 69 percent of Americans believe in the existence of angels, and 48 percent believe they have their own guardian angel. And 32 percent even said they have felt some kind of angelic presence in their life at some point.[2]

These statistics show us that, in a broad sense, Americans are a spiritual people and believe in an unseen supernatural world. Many of us believe in angels because we've probably had some close brush with death on at least one occasion, if not more. We've lived through a moment where we could have been easily killed — in an accident, on the job, or maybe in a car or motorcycle. And when it was over, after our pounding heart slowed down a little, we couldn't help but wonder: Did an angel intervene on my behalf?

Unfortunately, many, if not most, Americans have picked up their information and impressions about angels from the entertainment industry. And that's not usually a good thing. Over the years, Hollywood has hijacked the topic of angels, which has led to some significant distortions (to say the least). We looked at a few of them in the first chapter. For example, in the romantic 1998 movie *City of Angels*, Nicolas Cage plays an angel who falls in love with Meg Ryan. In the end, he decides to give up his rights as an angel and become a human. I can assure you that no such possibility even exists.

As a result of the liberties that pop culture takes with this subject, we acquire strange ideas that angels are exalted humans, or have to earn their wings, or any number of off-the-wall beliefs, to the point that although we say we believe in angels, what we believe in bears little resemblance to the biblical reality. But if we are going to understand Heaven, we are going to have to understand angels.

Lisa Miller contrasts the many sentimental and inaccurate portrayals of angels in the popular culture with the older understanding of these heavenly beings:

> Angels have been thought to live in heaven at least since the days of the Hebrew Bible, when God sent them to earth — notably to Abraham and Moses, then later, in the New Testament, to Mary, mother of Jesus — to convey His messages. These were not the winged cherubs of Hallmark cards, but splendid-and-petrifying agents of the Lord who prompt stammers of fear and disbelief from those who encounter them. "For beauty is nothing," the poet Rainer Maria Rilke wrote, echoing Old Testament authors,
>
> The beginning of terror, which we are still just able to endure,
> And we are so awed because it serenely disdains
> To annihilate us. Every angel is terrifying.[3]

I don't know that I agree with all of what she says, but there is some truth there. Perhaps this terrifying presence of angels is why usually the first thing they say to human onlookers is, "Do not be afraid." Perhaps this is also why they appear so rarely. Angels are not available for sale at the local gift shop as cute little porcelain figurines. They are beings of mystery, holiness, beauty, and power. No wonder "every angel is terrifying."

In fact, there is only one reliable source of information on angels, and that is Scripture. And it turns out that the Bible has quite a lot to say about them. Did you know that there are at least three hundred references to angels in the Old and New Testaments? In these passages, God pulls back the curtain a little and allows us to see angels — Heaven's messengers — at work in the lives of believers. And often angels do more than deliver God's messages. Sometimes they deliver God's people.

Acts 12 recounts when Simon Peter was arrested for preaching the gospel. The church is earnestly praying for him, and God dispatches an angel to deliver the imprisoned apostle. Peter, however, is so deeply asleep that the angel has to practically shake and punch him to get him moving. After that, the heavenly rescuer leads Peter right through the prison doors and gates (that open automatically for them) and into the street, a free man.

Or consider the amazing case of Daniel, who is a senior advisor to King Darius, the Mede. He has been advising the kings of Babylon and Medo-Persia for many years, with great wisdom and integrity. By now he is an old man. Abundantly blessed by God and in high favor with the king, Daniel also has enemies. Failing to come up with any dirt on Daniel, we learn in chapter 6 that they decide to use Daniel's well-known custom of praying three times a day against him. He would open up the shutters of his house, get down on his knees, and call on the Lord. They say, in effect, "Let's get a law passed that says no one can pray to any god except the king, and if you violate this law you are thrown into a den of lions. It has to work! Because we all know Daniel's going to keep right on praying."

And, as you probably know, he does, and they entrap him for it and have him thrown into the proverbial lions' den. However, there is someone else in that den who protects Daniel. When, the next morning, the anxious king inquires as to his welfare, Daniel replies, "O king, live forever! My God sent his angel and shut the lions' mouths, and they have not harmed me, because I was found blameless before him; and also before you, O king, I have done no harm" (Dan. 6:21-22). An angel protected him.

Maybe you find yourself in something like a lion's den right now. You're surrounded by hostile people or are facing overwhelming odds.

Remember the angel in the lions' den. The Lord is with you in your dark, confined space, as surely as He was with Daniel. And His angels will protect you until it's time for you to head home to Heaven.

The activity of angels, especially in the lives of believers, is constant. We may not be aware of their presence, or be able to predict how and where they might appear, but the Bible says that we can count on the fact that they're there—and perhaps nearer than we ever imagined.

Angels don't just show up every once in a while. They actually "hang out" with us, unseen but nevertheless close at hand. Psalm 34:7 says, "The angel of the LORD encamps around those who fear him, and delivers them."

Do you remember the story when Jacob is on his way home, scared spitless about meeting his estranged brother, Esau? "Jacob went on his way, and the angels of God met him. And when Jacob saw them he said, 'This is God's camp!' So he called the name of that place Mahanaim" (Gen. 32:1-2).

If we could only see, as Gehazi was privileged to see, then we would understand that we're *always* in God's camp. We may not be able to travel to Heaven, but Heaven's armies are more than willing to come to us and set up their tent, so to speak.

And when they get here, angels have a special work to accomplish in the lives of believers. Hebrews 1:14 tells us that angels are "ministering spirits sent out to serve for the sake of those who are to inherit salvation." We witness angels rescuing Lot and his family from the destruction of Sodom (see Gen. 19:16), for example.

In Billy Graham's classic book *Angels: God's Secret Agents*, we learn about John G. Paton, a nineteenth-century missionary to the New Hebrides Islands, where cannibals held sway. On one particular night, Paton and his wife were in their home at the mission station and got word of an imminent attack by an indigenous group. Knowing this, John and his wife began to pray. Hours passed, however, and all was peaceful; no attack ever came. The next morning, there was no sign of their enemies, and the missionary couple wondered what had happened.

A year or so later, the chief of the tribe that had wanted to kill the Patons received Jesus Christ as his Savior. One day, John said to him, "I have to ask you what happened that night when you were coming to kill us. Why didn't you follow through on it?" The chief replied, "What do you mean, why didn't we go through with it? Who were all of those men there with you?"

"There were no men there," Paton replied.

But the chief would have none of it. "We didn't attack," he said, "because there were hundreds of big men in shining garments with drawn swords, circling the mission station."

And in that moment, John knew that he and his wife had been guarded by a contingent of angels.[4]

Yes, angels are "God's secret agents." In other words, they're an elite fighting force, like the Navy Seals. When the Seals are dispatched on a mission, they go in, take care of business, and (until Osama bin Laden) you never hear about it. Well, angels are sent on missions all the time. They are "ministering spirits" who protect, deliver, guide, and bring messages from God to His people. You don't need to engage them, and you don't need to try to communicate with them. Just step back and let them do their jobs, the work that God has called them to do.

If an angel were to appear before you at this very moment, your temptation would be to worship him. That's exactly what happened to the apostle John (see Rev. 19:10; 22:9)—a guy you'd think would know better! Psalm 103:20 (KJV) tells us that they "excel in strength." Angels aren't as powerful as God, but they are vastly more powerful than we are.

I think we would be stunned beyond words if we could see how often (and how many) angels become involved in our day-to-day lives. John tells us that he saw "myriads of myriads and thousands of thousands" of angels around the throne (Rev. 5:11). In other words, he saw *millions* of angels.

There is a fascinating story in Daniel 10, when the prophet is fasting and praying. Daniel, an exile in the Persian Empire, sees a fearsome vision and collapses. After quite a delay, an angel—"his face like the appearance of lightning" (v. 6)—finally shows up to explain it to him.

> Fear not, Daniel, for from the first day that you set your heart to understand and humbled yourself before your God, your words have been heard, and I have come because of your words. The prince of the kingdom of Persia withstood me twenty-one days, but Michael, one of the chief princes, came to help me, for I was left there with the kings of Persia, and came to make you understand what is to happen to your people in the latter days. For the vision is for days yet to come. (vv. 12-14)

To paraphrase: "Daniel, I have to tell you why there seems to be a delay in the answer to your prayer. I was dispatched from Heaven twenty-one days ago with an answer, but I was opposed by a powerful fallen spirit identified as the Prince of Persia. I couldn't handle him, so Michael came and overpowered that demon entity, and I was free to then come and bring you the answer to your prayer."

Among other things, this account underlines the fact that angels have different rankings, and some are more powerful than others. (Michael, it seems, is *very* powerful.) But it also reminds us that when we pray, our prayers may unleash an invisible spiritual battle, and that the so-called delay to our prayers may be due at times to angelic battles going on behind the scenes—in the heavenlies, if you will.

So please hear this: When you are praying for someone's salvation, or when you are praying for a prodigal son or daughter to repent, *don't give up*. You have no idea what is happening behind the scenes, in the spirit world, as you pray. Don't just assume that God is turning down your prayer because the answer doesn't come quickly. He might be saying "no" today, but maybe He will say "yes" tomorrow, or the day after. It may take some time before His will is done on earth as it is in Heaven. Just keep praying!

Jesus said, "And I say unto you, Ask, and it shall be given you; seek, and ye shall find; knock, and it shall be opened unto you" (Lk. 11:9, KJV).

A more accurate translation of the original language, however, has this sense: *Keep on* asking. *Keep on* seeking. *Keep on* knocking. God's delays are not necessarily His denials.

As you're no doubt aware, 3D movies have made a big comeback. What if we could put on glasses that would allow us to see into the spiritual dimension, and watch angels and demons battle? It would be glorious, yes, but also terrifying. One day a great clash between Michael and the Devil (a fallen angel) will take place.

> War arose in heaven, Michael and his angels fighting against the dragon. And the dragon and his angels fought back, but he was defeated, and there was no longer any place for them in heaven. And the great dragon was thrown down, that ancient serpent, who is called the devil and Satan, the deceiver of the whole world — he was thrown down to the earth, and his angels were thrown down with him. (Rev. 12:7-9)

Michael and Satan are not the only angels whose names we know. Another is Gabriel, who appears in both the Old and New Testaments. In Daniel, he appears to the prophet with a revelation of the future. A voice between the banks of the Ulai River in Babylon calls out, "Gabriel, make this man understand the vision." Gabriel goes to Daniel and says, "Understand, O son of man, that the vision is for the time of the end" (Dan. 8:16-17). While Daniel is praying for the people, Gabriel shows up again, bringing the famous prophecy of the Seventy Weeks: "The man Gabriel, whom I had seen in the vision at the first, came to me in swift flight at the time of the evening sacrifice" (9:21).

Gabriel also shows up at another critical juncture, to tell Zechariah that his aged wife, Elizabeth, will bear John the Baptist (see Luke 1) and Mary that she will be pregnant with the Messiah. An interesting detail that Gabriel gives Zechariah is this: "I stand in the presence of God, and I was sent to speak to you and to bring you this good news" (1:19). Gabriel, one of God's secret agents, gets his orders directly from the heavenly Commander-in-Chief before he goes on this mission of utmost importance.

Do you remember when Moses came down from Mount Sinai and had to cover his face because it was shining after he had been in the presence of God (see Ex. 34:29-35)? Imagine the glowing countenance of an angel who "always sees" the face of God the Father (see Mt. 18:10)! This puts into perspective the statement of David: "As for me, I shall behold your face in righteousness; when I awake, I shall be satisfied with your likeness" (Ps. 17:15). David wants to do as the angels do. Seeing the face of God is, in many ways, the goal of every follower of Jesus Christ and the answer to all our longings. Theologians call it the "beatific vision."

The angels and those who have gone on to Heaven before us have the unspeakable privilege of experiencing the face of God right now. Whatever else Heaven offers — and all this is beyond human comprehension — it holds out the incredible promise that we too will one day see the *face of God*. This prospect should deepen and strengthen our anticipation of our "Heavenly reward," which, ultimately, is God Himself.

Other heavenly beings provide pictures of heavenly Reality. Cherubim and seraphim also inhabit Heaven. We don't know much about these awesome beings, but they too are angels. Interestingly, after Adam and Eve had been ejected from the Garden of Eden for eating the forbidden fruit, we read this statement: "[God] drove out the man, and at the east of the garden of Eden he placed the cherubim and a flaming sword that turned every way to guard the way to the tree of life" (Gen. 3:24).

The cherubim are not the chubby cherubs we see on Valentine's Day, but awesome creatures with four faces and four wings (see Ezk. 1:5-24; 10:2), although the cherubim used to adorn Ezekiel's vision of the temple had only two faces (see 41:8).[5] Cherubim are associated with the worship of God, appearing on the ark of the covenant (see Exodus 25; 37) and in Solomon's temple (see 1 K. 7:29; 36). They also participate in God's judgment.[6]

We have already read about the six-winged seraphim in Isaiah 6. Seraphim seem to be angels directly linked to the worship of God. In Isaiah's vision, a seraph provides atonement for the prophet's "unclean lips" with a burning coal from the altar (vv. 5-7).

Referring to Isaiah's vision of the Lord seated on His throne, John MacArthur notes that angelic worship of God is a clear signpost that angels have emotion: "Isaiah's description of these majestic creatures makes clear that they are not mere machines, or animals, but both highly intelligent and capable of the profoundest emotions associated with the highest kind of worship."[7] Not only this, but we will worship with the angels.

In a sense, we do this right now, of course. The great Christmas hymn "O Come, All Ye Faithful" contains the following exhortation to the angels to join us in adoring Christ:

Sing, choirs of angels, sing in exultation;
O sing, all ye citizens of Heaven above!
Glory to God, all glory in the highest.[8]

Such calls to worship remind us that just as adoration of God reflects the nature of unfallen angels, so it should characterize the souls of all redeemed men and women.

"Scripture indicates that in heaven we will join the angels in worshiping God around his throne," MacArthur says. "Revelation 4:4 describes the very first scene John witnessed in his vision of Heaven: 'Around the throne were twenty-four thrones, and seated on the thrones were twenty-four elders, clothed in white garments, with golden crowns on their heads.' . . . The fact that permanent seats are there for them indicates that the redeemed people of God will perpetually be worshiping there alongside the angels."[9]

The fact that angels perpetually worship the Lord, and we will one day join them in this worship, should say something significant to us about the indispensability of worshiping God now. Do we have the same passion for worshiping the Lord? Is His glory—in Heaven and on earth — our main concern? If not, what are we not seeing that *they* see?

Angels, of course, do more than instruct us by example. As we have seen, they become involved in our lives for God's glory and our good. But nowhere is angelic activity more powerful than in their participation with us in spreading the gospel. Acts 10 tells the fascinating story of when an angel appeared to Cornelius, a Roman centurion. Cornelius didn't yet know the Lord, but he seemed wide open to the things of God. The angel directed him to meet Simon Peter, who would give him the gospel.

Now why didn't the angel just do this himself? Why didn't this very knowledgeable and ultra-competent envoy from Heaven give Cornelius the gospel, instead of linking him up with a Christian who was miles away? Why? Because the primary mission of angels is not to preach the gospel. That is our job. They will help us do it, and they might even guide us in our efforts to do it. But God chooses to reach people primarily[10] through people.

Now if I were God, I don't think I would do it that way. It would seem more efficient just to use angels. Angels would always command attention, would always get their facts straight, and wouldn't get distracted or beat around the bush. They're never prejudiced or peevish, and they don't even get tired! But I'm not God (you can be thankful for that), and for whatever reason, He has chosen to reach people through other people, with angels working behind the scenes.

Another example of angelic direction occurs in Acts 8, when an angel directs Philip into the desert. Philip obeys, crossing paths with an Ethiopian official in a chariot who had come all the way to Jerusalem seeking knowledge of God. Philip presented the gospel to him, and the man came to faith in Christ.

Yes, the messengers of Heaven are definitely involved in our daily lives, on earth as it is in Heaven. As messengers of Heaven, sometimes they convey God's words of comfort or direction to us. Other times, angels may stop us from doing the wrong thing (as with Balaam) or guide us to do the right thing. They serve as powerful examples of the heavenly call to worship, and they assist us in helping give the good news to men and women, so that they too can go to Heaven.

But angels do one more thing I want to note here — they escort us, once our earthly life is past, *to* Heaven. In the story of Lazarus and the rich man, recall that Jesus said, "The poor man died and was carried by the angels to Abraham's side" (Lk. 16:22). This is a divine detail we need to take note of. Angels will take us into the presence of the Lord of Heaven. They are, in effect, the doormen of Heaven. What a privilege! Are you ready to be whisked into the presence of Jesus?

Some saints, however, receive even more special treatment in Heaven. Find out who they are . . . next.

CHAPTER 9

HEAVEN'S HEROES

Have you ever been persecuted for your faith in Christ, or do you know someone who has? I don't mean laughed at, ridiculed, or ignored. We all face that kind of opposition here in the West if we're willing to take a stand for Jesus, and it is indeed a low level form of persecution. But what I'm talking about is the possible loss of a friendship, your marriage, a job, your health, your money, or even your *life*—not because you were rude or thoughtless in how you shared the gospel, but *because you were a Christian*. That, my friend, is *persecution*.

And the apostle Paul, who suffered beatings, threats, imprisonment, and, ultimately, martyrdom, knew a little something about persecution. Paul warned us, "Yes, and everyone who wants to live a godly life in Christ Jesus will suffer persecution" (2 Tim. 3:12, NLT).

So even though it has become harder to be a Christian in a culture that glorifies sex without relationship or responsibility, "choice" without character, and "tolerance" without truth, we believers don't really grasp what true persecution is unless we make an effort. As a consequence, we feel disconnected from those who *are* persecuted. We have to work extra hard just to know what our fellow brothers and sisters in the faith experience in some parts of the world.

Organizations such as Open Doors or Voice of the Martyrs work full time to remind us of their plight in hard places such as Nigeria, Saudi Arabia, Vietnam, Iran, and North Korea so that we will pray, give, and advocate on their behalf. Here is part of a fairly typical report from Open Doors USA about what Christians can face in North Korea, which is run like a gigantic and ruthless religious cult:

> Open Doors has confirmed the recent deaths of two Christians in North Korea. One was shot while returning for Bible training in China. "He was very excited about his new faith and wanted to share the gospel with his family," says an Open Doors worker. "He wanted to come back to China to study the Bible more so he could explain the Christian faith better to his family. It is heartbreaking that he was killed."
>
> Another Christian recently died in a labor camp. This man had also studied the Bible in China.
>
> However, some arrested Christians face torture and then are released. The regime is hoping that they serve as bait to betray their families and other Christians.
>
> "This is extremely tragic," says one ministry worker. "It's so dangerous to help Christians who have been released by the government. Some have been tortured so severely they cannot walk anymore. Often we cannot help them, because that would bring too much risk to us. All we can do is pray for them. We know that Jesus will not leave them, nor forsake them."
>
> The number of trained North Korean spies inside China is growing. They are attempting to track down human rights activists and Christians helping North Korean refugees. Border patrols have been taken over by the North Korean National Security Agency, which pressures smugglers to turn in Christians in China who are helping defectors.
>
> In September 2011, a South Korean missionary was assassinated by North Korean agents. Another narrowly escaped. A South Korean pastor who was working for North Koreans in China, meanwhile, was killed in an unexplained car accident.
>
> So despite lack of attention that the global community is paying to their plight while nuclear fears grab the headlines, North Korean believers are grateful for the help and prayers of other believers. They are also firm in their faith.

One underground church leader wrote, in a letter smuggled out of the hermit kingdom, "No matter what circumstances we face, we stand firm in the mighty hands of God, and we will continue to march strongly towards the eternal kingdom."[1]

Well, you might be wondering, why is Laurie bringing up persecuted and martyred believers in a book about Heaven? In Heaven we can finally be done with all that ugly stuff and focus on worshiping and serving the Lord, right? And isn't it so that we probably won't even remember the suffering we experience for Christ? Won't God wipe away every tear?

As you'll recall, in the chapter on "What Heaven Knows About Earth," we looked at the idea that we in Heaven will have a "memory wipe" and concluded that we won't. We will indeed remember what happened to us and others on this planet. It's time to take a closer look at a particular aspect of what we will remember about earth when we are in Heaven. It has to do with persecution:

> When [the Lamb] opened the fifth seal, I saw under the altar the souls of those who had been slain for the word of God and for the witness they had borne. They cried out with a loud voice, "O Sovereign Lord, holy and true, how long before you will judge and avenge our blood on those who dwell on the earth?" Then they were each given a white robe and told to rest a little longer, until the number of their fellow servants and their brothers should be complete, who were to be killed as they themselves had been. (Rev. 6:9-11)

Despite the heroic work of advocacy groups such as Open Doors, the persecution of Christians for the sake of the gospel rarely, if ever, makes headlines here on earth. But it is all the buzz in Heaven. Revelation 6 describes a future time of chaos, danger, and judgment, when many will embrace the gospel in the midst of the most severe persecution the world has ever seen. It is a time of war, famine, and disease. Even the animal kingdom will turn on humanity (see v. 8).

Notice here that John the apostle is seeing all this chaos from Heaven. The saints in Heaven are also seeing it. And note something else about them: They are expressing a sort of heavenly impatience. They are not doubting God; they are freely calling Him "Sovereign Lord, holy and true." They trust God because they know His character, but they don't know His plan. They are longing for an end to the bloodshed.

Think of this for a moment. These slain saints are offering endless petitions for God to judge their persecutors. Sometimes we think that it is more godly to simply forgive and forget an offense than to cry out for judgment, but we see here in this heavenly scene that this is not necessarily the case.

Earlier in this book, we talked about the fact that people in Heaven will have a new perspective on the events of their lives. At a minimum, I think it is fair to say that in Heaven, sin will seem even more sinful to us. After all, the contrast between the light of God's (and our) holiness with the darkness of sin on earth will be even more stark. In Heaven, there will be no more gray areas. We will see the full heinousness of sin, in the same way that God sees it. We will abhor sin as God abhors it. There will be no more excuses, no more special pleadings.

The apostle Paul gives us a glimpse of this in explaining how God uses His law to reveal our sinfulness and our need for Him. You might think that the law was given to make us more holy, but, the truth is, it was given so that we could see how unholy we already are. The brightness of the Law shows the darkness of our hearts. It didn't *cause* that darkness—it *revealed* it, like a flashlight beam shining into the dark corners of an attic.

The Law was given to open our eyes and shut our mouths.

Paul says, "Did that which is good, then, bring death to me? By no means! It was sin, producing death in me through what is good, in order that sin might be shown to be sin, and through the commandment might become sinful beyond measure" (Ro. 7:13).

While there is no sin in Heaven, our heavenly perspective will enlighten us as to how the sins of earth are "sinful beyond measure" and must be judged. We will cry out for God's justice because we will want His will to be done on earth as it is in Heaven. The wonder is not when God judges sinful human beings, but when He forbears.

Of course, our God is a God of forgiveness, too, one who delights in forgiving us, who does everything out of His own infinite love (see 1 Jn. 4:8). When Moses asked God to see His face, the Lord stood before him on Mount Sinai and proclaimed His name: "The LORD, the LORD, a God merciful and gracious, slow to anger, and abounding in steadfast love and faithfulness, keeping steadfast love for thousands, forgiving iniquity and transgression and sin" (Ex. 34:6-7).

How we sometimes wish that the Lord had stopped there—but He didn't. The rest of the Lord's name puts that graciousness into context: "but who will by no means clear the guilty, visiting the iniquity of the fathers on the children and the children's children, to the third and the fourth generation" (34:7). God "will by no means clear the guilty"! When we hear this hard truth, we are forced to cry out with the disciples, "Then who can be saved?" (Lk. 18:26).

The good news is that God doesn't "clear" the guilty; He *forgives* us, by way of "the precious blood of Christ" (1 Pet. 1:19). He condemns every act of sin, but those of us who trust in Jesus have our sin punished at the cross. This is no cheap grace. Christ suffered God's holy and just wrath so we don't have to.

While on this earth it is right and good to pray and work for the salvation of all people, when we get to Heaven, we will cry out for God's justice on the unrepentant. We will do it because we will see sin for what it is, utterly sinful. We will also see God for Who He is: "Beloved, we are God's children now, and what we will be has not yet appeared; but we know that when he appears we shall be like him, because we shall see him as he is" (1 Jn. 3:2).

Those saints who suffer persecution and martyrdom on this planet are focused in Heaven on God's justice for themselves and for all who suffer unjustly "for the word of God and for the witness they had borne." This is no petty wish for revenge but a holy desire that good prevail over evil, on earth as it is in Heaven.

These saints who have been martyred for their faith are looking at the ongoing suffering below and saying to God, "How long, O Lord, holy and true, will You refrain from judging and avenging our blood on those who dwell on the earth?" (Rev. 6:10, NASB). They are saying, "Lord, an injustice is taking place. How long until you right the wrong? And how about our fellow brothers and sisters who are still suffering on earth?"

These saints under the altar know what it is like to suffer unjustly. They also know the Just One is poised to settle the score.

> The heavens and earth that now exist are stored up for fire, being kept until the day of judgment and destruction of the ungodly. But do not overlook this one fact, beloved, that with the Lord one day is as a thousand years, and a thousand years as one day. The Lord is not slow to fulfill his promise as some count slowness, but is patient toward you, not wishing that any should perish, but that all should reach repentance. (2 Pet. 3:7-9)

They call for justice because God is a God of justice.

Beyond the cry for justice, we also need to understand that the saints under the altar feel a powerful bond of camaraderie with each other in Heaven, with their still struggling fellow saints on earth, and with Jesus their forbearer in suffering for the truth. Christians in Heaven are bound in a mysterious way with those on the earth. While heavenly saints are part of the church in Heaven, compared with those earthly saints who are still part of the church on earth, we need to remember that we are all members of one body—the church universal.

These heavenly saints are still keenly interested in what happens with those they have left behind through martyrdom. So they ask, "How long will we have to watch? How long will the proud God-haters hold sway over the earth?" God's answer is given in Revelation 6:11: "And there was given to each of them a white robe; and they were told that they should rest for a little while longer, until *the number of* their fellow servants and their brethren who were to be killed even as they had been, would be completed also" (NASB).

These heavenly heroes know they were killed for following Jesus Christ. This shows a direct continuity between our identity on earth and our identity in Heaven. These are not different people. They are the same people relocated. These martyrs are fully conscious, rational, and aware of each other. They know they have been killed, and they want justice—for themselves, and for those to whom they still feel connected.

I was speaking to a lady who has a son with a severe disability. Caring for this boy has been an extremely difficult labor of love, but it has forced this dear woman to lift her eyes heavenward. Referring to her son, she told me, "His life has placed one of my feet in Heaven, and one on earth." She, like so many others in this life, is carrying a heavy load, and I quite naturally felt compassion for her.

But when you stop and think about it, having one foot in Heaven and the other on earth is not such a bad place to be. Pain and suffering can bring about this uneasy stance between two worlds, as can the unexpected death of a loved one. You long to see that person, such as what has happened to me with the unexpected loss of my son Christopher. In such cases, we feel connected to Heaven by stronger cords than we ever could have imagined.

In *Mere Christianity*, C. S. Lewis commended such hope as good and right. Lewis said, "This means that a continual looking forward to the eternal world is not (as some modern people think) a form of escapism or wishful thinking, but one of the things a Christian is meant to do."[2]

For the believer, death is not only the great separator; in Jesus Christ, death is the great uniter. When we get to Heaven, we will not only be reunited with those who have gone before us (even perhaps those who suffered for their faith), but we will be united with those who may have helped bring us to faith. In 1 Thessalonians 2:19-20 (NIV), the apostle writes: "For what is our hope, our joy, or the crown in which we will glory in the presence of our Lord Jesus when he comes? Is it not you? Indeed, you are our glory and joy."

I *love* that! Paul is saying that his spiritual children will be his crown of rejoicing in the Lord's presence when He comes. This passage seems to imply that when we get to Heaven, we will in some sense have grouped around us those we helped bring to faith in Jesus. Now maybe that thought actually discourages you a little, because you might be saying, "I don't know that I have really helped that many people believe in Jesus."

Certainly this should motivate us to reach as many people as we can with the gospel message. I want to bring as many people as possible to Heaven with me. But the fact is, you really don't know how many people you have helped along in their coming to faith in Jesus Christ. You haven't seen the big plan, and you don't know how touching one person's life ended up touching someone else's life and . . . on and on it goes. On this side of Heaven, you and I can't really know how it will all play out.

The important thing to keep in mind as we seek to do the Lord's will on earth as it is in Heaven is to simply be faithful with the opportunities that God sets before us. The truth is, you may have reached more people than you realize. After all, ultimately it is *God* who converts people, not you or me. We are certainly responsible to do our part, but the Bible says that one sows, another waters, but it is *God* who gives the increase (see 1 Cor. 3:6). God is the one who brings men and women into the kingdom of God. Isn't that comforting?

So how do we sow and water in evangelism? When you pray for the work of evangelism, you become invested in it. When you give financially to support the work of evangelism, you become invested in it. When you are kind to someone and help or bless someone in the name of Jesus, you become invested in evangelizing that life. In fact, Jesus said, "For truly, I say to you, whoever gives you a cup of water to drink because you belong to Christ will by no means lose his reward" (Mk. 9:41).

So what kinds of rewards are we talking about? While we will have an entire chapter on this important topic later in the book, I'll just mention one here: One of the rewards, one of the crowns we will receive, is the people whose lives we have touched for the gospel: "Is it not *you*?" As we've seen, one of the paradoxical things about God's economy is that while death breaks ties on earth, it renews them in Heaven. Thus, our joy will overflow!

In Matthew 17, Jesus appears on the Mount of Transfiguration with Moses and Elijah. Did you ever wonder how everyone knew they were Moses and Elijah, without their saying so? Do you think Moses was standing there with the stone tablets under his arm, or that maybe Elijah was calling down fire from Heaven? Or do you imagine they had those newcomer badges that people sometimes wear, that said, "Hi, I'm Moses," or, "Hi, I'm Elijah"? No, I don't think so. Somehow, they were simply recognizable, and the men on the mountain with Jesus that day knew instantly who they were.

I believe it will be the same for us in Heaven. Somehow, I don't think we will need lengthy introductions, "icebreakers," and get-acquainted sessions when we first arrive through the pearly gates. I love the way Jesus stated it after He rose from the dead and met with His followers. He said, "It is I myself! Touch me and see" (Lk. 24:39, NIV).

It's Me, guys. It wasn't a *different* Jesus. It was (and is) the same Jesus . . . in a glorified body.

You may or may not face persecution and martyrdom for being a Christian. Only God knows what's ahead for you, what cross you will have to bear. But *one* thing is for sure—you *will* face trials. I like to call them the storms of life. Sometimes these storms will be expected, and we watch them build and brew with great concern in our hearts. But at other times, storms seem to slam into our world out of nowhere, with no warning at all. Maybe it's a heart attack . . . or a rebellious child . . . or a pink slip at work . . . or a crumbling marriage. It might even be the death of someone you love very much. These sorts of storms can alter the very landscape of our lives.

Here is what you need to know about life storms in general: *You're going to have them.* There are really only two kinds of people in the world: those who are experiencing a crisis, and those who are about to experience a crisis. You're either in a storm or you're headed into one. Friend, that is not pessimism; that is *life.*

But we can have a heavenly perspective *above* the clouds of these storms, whether they have their origin in persecution or in something else. Persecution may, and probably will, become much more common in the Western church, and perhaps sooner rather than later. But even if it doesn't, a storm is coming. And whatever it is, we can act heroically. Yes, the storm will end for every child of God . . . but it may not end on this side of eternity. In Heaven, however, we will see the big picture and begin to understand God's ultimate plan and purpose for our lives.

Right now, though, as with our brothers and sisters above, who've fought the good fight of faith (see 1 Tim. 4:7), we can pray for God's justice. We can also pray for His joy, His endurance, and His wisdom in the midst of whatever storm comes our way. And as we do, we can know for certain that we have a heavenly cheering section, urging us on.

It is to this glorious truth that we now turn.

CHAPTER 10

A ROYAL
CHEERING SECTION

One of the biggest fears that many people have about death isn't facing the judgment of God (the subject of a later chapter), but simply being separated from loved ones. I shared some of my own journey in an earlier chapter about how I have come to terms with the death of my son Christopher. I have a sure hope that I will see him again because we are both trusting in Jesus.

Dinesh D'Souza takes note of this longing for reunion with loved ones who have "passed over" to the other side. He provides a short list of examples from ancient and recent history.

> In Shakespeare's *Julius Caesar*, Brutus receives a warning from the apparition of the dead Caesar, and in Charles Dickens' *A Christmas Carol*, Scrooge is taught a lesson by the ghost of Christmases past. Films like *Ghost* and *The Sixth Sense* provide glimpses both appealing and terrifying about what it might be like to communicate with those who have died. In nineteenth-century England and America, people sometimes consulted "mediums" to receive messages from dead relatives.[1]

Lisa Miller says that about half of all Americans believe they'll be reunited with loved ones when they die. She recounts the story of a meeting between Billy Graham and President Lyndon Johnson, a rough and ready Texan who suffered no fools and knew how to get what he wanted. But when it came to one day seeing loved ones who had died, LBJ was at a loss.

> The president and Graham are driving around Johnson's Texas ranch, and Johnson parks his car by the spot where his mother and father are buried beneath some shady oaks. He then turns to Graham and, after a pause filled with meaning, asks, "Billy, will I ever see my mother and father again?"
>
> "Well, Mr. President," Graham told him, "if you're Christian and they were Christians then someday you'll have a great homecoming."[2]

This concern was less prominent in earlier times. Augustine held that believers in the afterlife will be primarily focused on God, not on their relatives. Dante believed the same. "In Canto 32 of the Paradiso," Miller writes, "Dante describes Heaven as a kind of crowded stadium. Souls are arranged in rows; the holiest souls get the best seats, closest to the light, while the least worthy sit farthest away. No matter their rank, all are perfectly content—for all are engaged in the activity of Heaven, which is gazing upon God."[3]

Interestingly enough, the book of Hebrews suggests a heavenly stadium scene, but the focus of the spectators is not on what you might expect. In this scene, they are looking at neither God *nor* at one another. Instead, similar to the martyred saints of Revelation 6, it appears they are looking at *us*:

> Since we are surrounded by so great a cloud of witnesses, let us also lay aside every weight, and sin which clings so closely, and let us run with endurance the race that is set before us, looking to Jesus, the founder and perfecter of our faith, who for the joy that was set before him endured the cross, despising the shame, and is seated at the right hand of the throne of God. (Heb. 12:1-2)

These spectators constitute a "great cloud of witnesses" as we run the race of the Christian life. Now this verse may be saying these witnesses are primarily examples. In other words, they have lived godly lives that we should emulate. That certainly is true, but could it also be true that Scripture is telling us they are seeing us from Heaven?

Notice also that Hebrews 12:1 says that we are "surrounded" by these witnesses as *we* run. It is hard to miss the idea that we're in a stadium, surrounded by cheering fans. Or think about a marathon. Many times, after the fastest runners cross the finish line, they stick around to cheer on those who are bringing up the rear. The point is not to see who *won* the race, but to celebrate everyone who *finishes*.

In June 2012, something even more extraordinary happened. At a track meet for high school girls at Jesse Owens Stadium in Columbus, Ohio, runner Meghan Vogel, a junior from West Liberty-Salem High School, saw a competitor, sophomore Arden McMath of Arlington High School, collapse in front of her, just 20 meters from the finish line. Other runners might have just sprinted on, but not Meghan. She stopped, helped Arden get up, and carried her to the finish line, making sure *Arden* crossed first.

"Any girl on the track," Meghan said, "would have done the same for me."[4]

As this act of selflessness shows, often there is great camaraderie among runners. If that's true in a mere footrace, think of how much more true it is with the body of Christ and "the race that is set before us."

But what constitutes running a good race for the Christian?

Everyone knows that the Olympic Games started in Greece. Back then, Nike, meaning "victory," was a god the people worshiped, not a shoe they wore! At the end of the race, a crown of laurel leaves—not a gold medal—would be given to the winner. As you were coming down the stretch, you could see your reward and the one holding it. That sight gave you the added motivation to finish well.

The King James Version speaks of our being "compassed about with so great a cloud of witnesses." I love that archaic wording! A compass, of course, is a round instrument with a needle that gives us our bearings. These witnesses are encompassing us. They surround us on every side. Who are these witnesses? Are they possibly the loved ones who have gone on before us, cheering us on from the grandstands of Heaven? I think that is a distinct possibility. I often wonder whether Christopher, having gone before me, is in those stands right now, cheering me on. What a sweet possibility, especially when I consider our lives together — now temporarily sundered.

When Christopher was just a boy and I would carry him around, he was always a curious little guy, and he would point to things and ask me what they were. And because he was very little, he didn't say, "What's that?" He just said, "S'at."

He would point to a truck. "S'at — ?"

"That's a truck."

"S'at — ?"

"That's a tree."

"S'at — ?"

"That's another tree."

"S'at — ?"

"That's a house."

He said it over and over: *S'at, S'at, S'at,* until it really began to wear me out.

So now, Topher (his nickname) has gone on to Heaven ahead of me. And after I arrive and we're walking around together, I will say,

"S'at — ?"

"That's the sea of glass, Dad."

"S'at — ?"

"That's an angel, Dad."

"When do we eat dinner?"

"Anytime, Dad."

But there will be other saints in Heaven, too, as the context shows. Hebrews 12, of course, follows Hebrews 11, which many have described as "the hall of faith." It's something of a "who's who" of God's all-stars. In the first verse of Hebrews 12, the writer seems to be saying, "In light of the fact that these men and women of God served the Lord so faithfully, you'd better run a good race, too." Who are these old saints in Heaven who are cheering us on in our own race on earth, and what can we learn from them? Let's take a quick tour of some of those the author of Hebrews specifically names in chapter 11. And let's keep in mind that everything they did, they did "by faith."

Abel (Heb. 11:4) "offered to God a more acceptable sacrifice" and paid for it with his life (see Gen. 4:1-8). As we saw in the previous chapter, martyrs for the faith have a special place near God in Heaven, as well as a keen interest in suffering fellow believers here on earth. One of those heavenly martyrs cheering on the suffering is Abel, who gave his very best to the Lord, and then ended up giving his life. Are we willing to give our all, even our lives, for the kingdom? Isn't Heaven worth it? Isn't *God*?

Enoch, we have already observed, "walked with God." Hebrews 11:5 says he was "taken up" because he "pleased God." Enoch was a "God pleaser" rather than a "people pleaser." The Bible has plenty of encouragement for us to avoid being people pleasers and instead be God pleasers:

- Am I now seeking the approval of man, or of God? Or am I trying to please man? If I were still trying to please man, I would not be a servant of Christ. (see Gal. 1:10)
- Slaves, obey in everything those who are your earthly masters, not by way of eye-service, as people-pleasers, but with sincerity of heart, fearing the Lord. Whatever you do, work heartily, as for the Lord and not for men, knowing that from the Lord you will receive the inheritance as your reward. You are serving the Lord Christ. (see Col. 3:22-24)
- Beware of practicing your righteousness before other people in order to be seen by them, for then you will have no reward from your Father who is in Heaven. (see Mt. 6:1)

And what a reward Enoch received for pleasing God and not men! "By faith," Hebrews 11:5 tells us, "Enoch was taken up so that he should not see death." Yes, Enoch pleased God. His focus was on his Father in Heaven, and that's where he ended up. Where's *your* focus?

Noah "in reverent fear constructed an ark for the saving of his household. By this he condemned the world and became an heir of the righteousness that comes by faith" (Heb. 11:7). Noah took the most unpopular stand imaginable. He condemned the whole world. This was no quick decision on Noah's part. It must have taken years for Noah and his family to construct an ark 450 feet long, 75 feet wide, and 45 feet high.

Noah no doubt considered his situation, the weather, and his standing in the community as he worked. I expect he endured a ton of ridicule and hostility from his neighbors far and wide. "Where is the rain, Noah?" they may have jeered as the antediluvian sun kept shining. "How are you going to get that thing into the water?" Yet he stuck with it, "a preacher of righteousness" the whole time (2 Pet. 2:5, NIV). And when the flood finally came, Noah's faith was rewarded. How about *you*? Do you have that kind of perseverance for the Lord? Remember, Noah may be cheering you on from Heaven right now.

Then we have witnesses Abraham and Sarah:

By faith Abraham obeyed when he was called to go out to a place that he was to receive as an inheritance. And he went out, not knowing where he was going. By faith he went to live in the land of promise, as in a foreign land, living in tents with Isaac and Jacob, heirs with him of the same promise. For he was looking forward to the city that has foundations, whose designer and builder is God. By faith Sarah herself received power to conceive, even when she was past the age, since she considered him faithful who had promised. Therefore from one man, and him as good as dead, were born descendants as many as the stars of heaven and as many as the innumerable grains of sand by the seashore. (Heb. 11:8-12)

The first thing this passage says about Abraham is that he *obeyed*. Yes, he obeyed "by faith," but he *obeyed*. As James 2:17 says, "So also faith by itself, if it does not have works, is dead." We cannot say we have true faith if we never have works, and what work is more basic than doing what God says? Consider Abraham's situation. God told him to leave Haran, but He didn't even tell Abraham where they were headed.

Most of us want a roadmap or a well-planned itinerary before we will go on a trip of any length. We make sure the GPS is working, the tires are aired up, and there's gas in the tank. Abraham didn't have any of that. All he had was trust and an unknown future.

But Abraham had a known God so he obeyed. Do you always need for God to explain everything to you first? Abraham didn't, because he trusted the character of the Lord. Do *we*? And the passage tells us he had to rough it, living in tents, looking forward ultimately to a city with foundations — Heaven itself.

Sarah, meanwhile, was simply asked to do the impossible — to have a baby well past childbearing age. She, too, had to wait for many long years, but God rewarded her and Abraham's imperfect faith with a child named Isaac. Isaac was the first link in a chain that led to the entire world being blessed. Abraham even offered back his hard-won blessing to God, trusting that the Lord would provide (see Heb. 11:19). Are we willing to patiently obey and wait for God's blessings the way Abraham and Sarah did? Whatever your race in life, whatever you are being asked to wait for, remember: Abraham and Sarah did it, and so can you.

Isaac, the son of God's promise, looked forward in faith as he blessed Jacob and Esau (see Heb. 11:20; Gen. 27:1-45). Though Jacob and Rebekah had tricked Isaac, his seemingly misdirected blessings were part of God's sovereign plan for the people of God all along. Do we, like cheering Isaac, have faith to trust in the Lord's workings in our lives even when we can't clearly see the path ahead?

By the end of his years, a dying *Jacob*, who was a trickster most of his life, blessed his sons, "bowing in worship over the head of his staff" (Heb. 11:21; see Gen. 48:8-22). Jacob reminds us, perhaps from the stands of Heaven, that it's not how you start; it's how you finish. By faith and by God's grace, Jacob finished well. Though he was on his deathbed, Jacob could still give glory to God. He didn't need to do anything else, and there wasn't anything more important than this, anyway.

Friend, you or a loved one may be near the end, with the other side of the Jordan in view. You may barely be able to keep your head up or your eyes open. That's all right. Someday, unless the Lord returns first, we'll *all* be there. Exercise your faith in spite of your struggles. The Lord has you here for a reason. Give glory to God. Don't worry about the rest. It is enough. Remember, whatever the race marked out for you, "The LORD cares deeply when his loved ones die" (Ps. 116:15, NLT).

By faith *Joseph*, also at death's door, "made mention of the exodus of the Israelites and gave directions concerning his bones" (Heb. 11:22). Joseph had seen it all and done it all. Left for dead by his jealous brothers, he became a prisoner, then a slave, then second-in-command over all Egypt, providing for God's people in the midst of a killer famine.

But Joseph's heart was back in the Promised Land all along. His agenda was not his own. He knew God was going to bless the Israelites and return them to their land. He knew of God's plan to bless the world through them. And he knew he wanted to be a part of that plan — even posthumously. Joseph had ridden the career escalator all the way to the top, but he was willing to be buried with God's people.

Let me ask you: Whose agenda are you following? Your own, or another's? You can tell by where your heart is. As Jesus said, "No one can serve two masters" (Mt. 6:24). Few saints know this truth better than Joseph, the great leader who was a slave to the God of the universe.

Then we come to *Moses*:

> By faith Moses, when he was born, was hidden for three months by his parents, because they saw that the child was beautiful, and they were not afraid of the king's edict. By faith Moses, when he was grown up, refused to be called the son of Pharaoh's daughter, choosing rather to be mistreated with the people of God than to enjoy the fleeting pleasures of sin. He considered the reproach of Christ greater wealth than the treasures of Egypt, for he was looking to the reward.

By faith he left Egypt, not being afraid of the anger of the king, for he endured as seeing him who is invisible. By faith he kept the Passover and sprinkled the blood, so that the Destroyer of the firstborn might not touch them. (Heb. 11:23-28)

Moses was another luminary in Egypt who chose God's people and God's agenda over the world's prestige and power. "He considered the reproach of Christ greater wealth than the treasures of Egypt," the writer says, "for he was looking to the reward." Though God was "invisible" to his physical eyes, Moses' faith in the coming Messiah was not blind. Moses, a prince of Egypt, made a cool and determined calculation that what he was giving up, "the treasures of Egypt," couldn't hold a candle to what he was embracing — "the reward." Randy Alcorn says we need to make the same choice in light of our heavenly home in eternity.

There's nothing wrong with having money. We need it to live while we're still living in this foreign land away from home, and God graciously provides it for us. Still, we must understand its limits. Like Confederate money near the end of the Civil War, it's only good for a very short period of time, and that time is running out. It will be worthless once we get home.[5]

Moses understood the limits of earthly money in contrast with our heavenly reward. It took faith to see that truth then. It takes faith now, too. That's why people like Moses are up there right now, cheering us on. I can almost hear them urging us on toward the finish line. "It's not that much farther! You're almost there! Don't give up!"

But our main spectator in Heaven is Jesus. Hebrews 12:2 says we are to be "looking to Jesus, the founder and perfecter of our faith." We run for an audience of One. While we can certainly draw encouragement and instruction from other saints for our own race of faith, the fact is, Jesus is our ultimate inspiration. He ran the race for us, died on the cross in our place, and was raised so that we could one day join

Him in Heaven. He gave up all to give us all. Through His poverty we become rich (see 2 Cor. 8:9).

From Heaven, Jesus is saying to His fellow runners remaining on the earth, "Come on! You can make it! Keep going! Follow Me!" Listen, we don't know when life is going to end. We don't know when we are going to be among the number in the stadium on the other side. We do know, however, that it will be a glorious gathering. Here's what the rest of the chapter says about our heavenly finish line.

> You have not come to what may be touched, a blazing fire and darkness and gloom and a tempest and the sound of a trumpet and a voice whose words made the hearers beg that no further messages be spoken to them. For they could not endure the order that was given, "If even a beast touches the mountain, it shall be stoned." Indeed, so terrifying was the sight that Moses said, "I tremble with fear." But you have come to Mount Zion and to the city of the living God, the heavenly Jerusalem, and to innumerable angels in festal gathering, and to the assembly of the firstborn who are enrolled in heaven, and to God, the judge of all, and to the spirits of the righteous made perfect, and to Jesus, the mediator of a new covenant, and to the sprinkled blood that speaks a better word than the blood of Abel. (Heb. 12:18-24)

The writer is contrasting the Old Testament understanding of life with God with the even better New Testament revelation of the "city with foundations." Alluding to God's awesome presence with Moses on Sinai — a fearsome scene with fire, gloom, and trumpet blasts — the passage says we have come home to a new mountain, "Mount Zion and to the city of the living God, the heavenly Jerusalem, and to innumerable angels in festal gathering, and to the assembly of the firstborn who are enrolled in heaven, and to God, the judge of all, and to the spirits of the righteous made perfect, and to Jesus, the mediator of a new covenant."

Picture the scene. Instead of judgment, we get joy; instead of the old covenant, we get the new. There are "innumerable" angels, of course, but also "the spirits of the righteous made perfect." How big must the heavenly stadium be?

It is a huge pep rally, if you will, one we can join today. John MacArthur notes, "Our departed loved ones in the faith are with Christ and with the Father. Every Old and New Testament believer who has died is now in Heaven."[6]

When I travel, I start missing home almost as soon as I leave the ground. If you are overseas very long, you long for your country, you long for your house, you long for your bed, and you certainly long for your family. Well, let me remind you that you are traveling *now*. Your real home is elsewhere, and so is your heavenly family. They're *up there*. Are you longing for them? Perhaps you can hear your brothers and sisters in the faith cheering you on, however faintly, right now.

And maybe, just maybe, you can hear their celebrating for another special reason, which we'll turn to in the next chapter.

CHAPTER 11

PARTY TIME

Billy Graham was a few days short of sixteen. He and a friend, Grady Wilson, went to a crusade conducted by the evangelist Mordecai Ham in Charlotte, North Carolina. Graham was both drawn to and repelled by what he saw. Graham had never seen such a big crowd and was fascinated.

On the other hand, Ham was an intimidating preacher. As he jabbed his index finger to make his points, Graham and Wilson became increasingly uncomfortable. The young Billy didn't like being told he was headed for Hell. The boys felt as if Ham were speaking directly to them.

"Two young high school boys attended our meeting," Ham later recalled. "They thought that everything I said was directed their way; so they decided to take seats in the choir, where I couldn't point my finger at them. They didn't pretend to be singers, but they wanted to be behind me."

Wilson later admitted, "Neither of us could sing."

At the end of the first meeting, Graham said, "I am through!" But what Ham the evangelist had said stuck with him that night and all the next day, and he was back again, saying later, "I couldn't get there soon enough the next night!"

Ham recounted, "One night a man spoke to them during the invitation and said, 'Come on; let's go up front.' Billy and Grady both went to the altar. Billy was saved, and Grady dedicated his life to Christian service."[1] It was November 1, 1935 . . . a date that would change the world.

We all know what Billy Graham has accomplished around the world in his life and ministry, but few of us are familiar with Mordecai Ham, whose ministry was instrumental in bringing the teenager to Christ. Ham, a regional evangelist, was invited to Charlotte by a Christian businessmen's association that had been founded after an evangelistic campaign ten years earlier by the prominent national evangelist Billy Sunday, a former professional baseball player and colorful anti-liquor crusader who once famously said, "Sin can be forgiven, but stupid is forever."

Before his own preaching ministry began, Sunday briefly worked for evangelist J. Wilbur Chapman, who worked with the great Chicago evangelist D. L. Moody, who received Christ as Lord and Savior after speaking with Edward Kimball, a co-worker with Moody selling shoes.

Who would have thought that one man — a Sunday school teacher at that — could have had such a global impact? Do you think that Kimball himself had any inkling when he was speaking about Jesus with young Moody what the ultimate outcome would be? That young D. L. Moody would go from selling soles to saving souls?

I've mentioned the movie *It's a Wonderful Life* already, and one quote from it seems appropriate here. After Clarence shows George Bailey all the positive influence he has had on so many people in Bedford Falls (and the tragedy left by his absence), the angel says, "Strange, isn't it? Each man's life touches so many other lives. When he isn't around he leaves an awful hole, doesn't he?"[2]

Few of us are privileged to touch as many lives as Billy Graham has, but there's not a one of us who probably can't identify, at least a little bit, with Edward Kimball. Could it be that your faithful testimony and consistent witness — in a Sunday school class, in your neighborhood, at the office, or by your mom or dad's bedside — may reach hundreds or even thousands of people over the decades? Only God knows, of course, but however many people it is, we know that Heaven itself rejoices each and every time a sinner turns to Christ. We know this because Jesus Himself says so.

Earlier in this book, we looked at the connection of concern and fellowship between those who had lost their lives for being Christians —

those who are now in Heaven—and those still suffering for their faith on the earth. Then, in the previous chapter, we talked about the royal cheering section in Heaven that we all have as we run the daily race for Jesus. Well, in this chapter, we'll consider another connection between Heaven and earth that will encourage us in one of the most critical aspects of the Christian life—evangelism.

I don't know about you, but I tend to lose things. The older I get, the more I lose. It is kind of embarrassing when you lose your car. Sometimes I have a severe case of Mallzheimer's disease, unable to locate my vehicle in the parking lot. The only time I ever use the red emergency button on my keychain is when I am trying to find my car! I will listen for that comforting beeping sound, track down the car—usually one level up—get in, and drive home, hoping no one saw me. Maybe you lose things, too.

Sometimes, however, losing things is not at all funny. Sometimes it's terribly serious—even a matter of life and death. Have you ever "lost" the combination to a lock or a safety deposit box? Maybe the thumb drive where you store all your passwords has gone AWOL. Perhaps you've had your identity stolen. It's a sick, panicky feeling we get when we can no longer get to those things that are ours.

Think about how much worse it is when you are at a park or a shopping center with one of your kids. You get distracted by something, look away for a few minutes, and, when you turn back, your child is gone! You'll drop everything—even the groceries in your arms—and risk looking foolish until you can find your little boy or girl. Nothing matters except finding your child . . . nothing.

In Luke 15, Jesus tells three stories, all dealing with lost things. We will look at each in turn here. The Lord spoke them in response to the Pharisees and scribes, who were complaining that Jesus was spending time with the dregs of first-century Jewish society. Why wasn't He hanging out with the important, "holy" people instead? "The tax collectors and sinners were all drawing near to hear him. And the Pharisees and the scribes grumbled, saying, 'This man receives sinners and eats with them'" (vv. 1-2).

Jesus' answer tells us something important about what Heaven's priorities are and what ours should be too. The first story describes a shepherd who has lost a sheep.

> He told them this parable: "What man of you, having a hundred sheep, if he has lost one of them, does not leave the ninety-nine in the open country, and go after the one that is lost, until he finds it? And when he has found it, he lays it on his shoulders, rejoicing. And when he comes home, he calls together his friends and his neighbors, saying to them, 'Rejoice with me, for I have found my sheep that was lost.' Just so, I tell you, there will be more joy in heaven over one sinner who repents than over ninety-nine righteous persons who need no repentance." (vv. 3-7)

Here we read that when only *one* sheep goes astray, the shepherd leaves the other ninety-nine. Think about that for a minute. That sheep represents only 1 percent of the shepherd's wealth or responsibility—just a penny on the dollar. That's not very much, is it? Yet to the shepherd—and to God—that one sheep is worth all the time and trouble. Stan Guthrie tells the following story in his book *All That Jesus Asks*, about when he was doing a live call-in radio program about Christian-Jewish relations with Rabbi Yehiel Poupko in Chicago:

> [H]e asked me why Christians are so intent on converting the Jews, who probably constitute just 1 percent of the world's population. Why didn't we just leave his people alone and focus on the other 99 percent? I reminded him of the story that Jesus told the Pharisees and scribes, who were complaining that he was hanging out with sinners. . . .
>
> [In the parable] Jesus tells the elite that God cares about sinners, like a man determinedly seeking his helpless, lost sheep. He is willing—no, eager—to leave the 99 to find the one. God's math is not like ours. . . . God is willing to go out of his way to rescue the one, to trouble about it, to inconvenience himself, to search for it.[3]

The shepherd searches for the lost sheep until he finds it. Then he wraps it around his shoulders and returns home, rejoicing. And he says to his friends, "Rejoice with me, for I have found my sheep that was lost." Then Jesus gives the scribes and Pharisees the application: "Just so, I tell you, there will be more joy in heaven over one sinner who repents than over ninety-nine righteous persons who need no repentance."

These men were dismissive, or perhaps even secretly jealous, of the fact that the Lord was spending quality *and* quantity time with "sinners." Instead, He says, they ought to have thrown a party. Why? Because that's what happens in Heaven whenever someone trusts Christ! These religious "authorities" were busy telling others what Heaven was like and how to get there, but they actually had no clue about what was important in Heaven and how that knowledge ought to impact how we live on this earth. Here is the point: *When a person believes on earth, it is a big deal in Heaven.*

You see, when people believe in Jesus on earth, it is public knowledge in Heaven. It is such an important point that Jesus says it not once, not twice, but three separate ways. The first, of course, is about the shepherd who lost a sheep. The second is about a woman who lost a coin.

> What woman, having ten silver coins, if she loses one coin, does not light a lamp and sweep the house and seek diligently until she finds it? And when she has found it, she calls together her friends and neighbors, saying, "Rejoice with me, for I have found the coin that I had lost." Just so, I tell you, there is joy before the angels of God over one sinner who repents. (Lk. 15:8-10)

Like the shepherd, the woman has lost something extremely valuable to her—in her case, a coin, which represents *10* percent of her wealth. (How much would that be for you?) Back in those days, instead of a wedding ring, a woman would wear a wedding band like a headband. And in the headband would be coins. To lose one from your headband was the equivalent of losing your wedding ring. She doesn't write it off, content with the nine she still has. No, she gets to work, lighting a lamp and getting out the broom.

Have you ever been in similar straits? Of *course* you have! We all have lost *something*—maybe a bill, a tool, or a driver's license—and then had to search feverishly until we found it. We couldn't eat, couldn't sleep, and couldn't even watch TV (that's a joke) until it turned up. Not having that precious thing gave us a sick feeling in the pits of our stomachs!

Do you remember the scene in the film version of *The Fellowship of the Ring* when Bilbo loses the Ring and tears apart his hobbit hole looking for it—finally discovering it, safe and sound, in his breast pocket? If so, then you know what this woman would have felt upon losing and finding her coin. No wonder she throws a party!

Again, Jesus spells out the lesson: "Just so, I tell you, there is joy before the angels of God over one sinner who repents." Heaven is rejoicing that these "sinners" are entering the kingdom, Jesus says. Why aren't the scribes and Pharisees? Heavenly priorities, Jesus implies, need to be our priorities . . . on earth as it is in Heaven. So if our conversion is such a big deal in Heaven, shouldn't it also be a big deal on earth?

And if conversion is a heavenly priority, what does this say about evangelism as an earthly priority? As the apostle Paul asks, "How then will they call on him in whom they have not believed? And how are they to believe in him of whom they have never heard? And how are they to hear without someone preaching?" (Ro. 10:14).

But I want you to notice something *else* that Jesus says here: "There is joy before the angels," or, as the King James Version puts it, "in the presence of the angels." It doesn't say that there is joy *among* the angels. Now I am not saying that angels *don't* rejoice when people come to Christ. They probably do. But He didn't say there is joy *among* the angels. He said, "There is joy in the *presence* of the angels." That makes me wonder if the joy He is talking about is experienced by those who are already in Heaven—that is, those believers who have already died.

Think about this for a moment. Could some of these celebrating saints who counted the cost of following Jesus be those to whom you witnessed? Might you be their Mordecai Ham or D. L. Moody? Could it be that your faithful testimony and consistent witness may, through the interlocking elements of God's gracious plan, reach hundreds and perhaps even thousands of people before it's all over? If the Lord does not return before you die, have you considered that perhaps you yourself will be in Heaven to see someone else's faith come alive when it matters the most?

I don't want to be too dogmatic here, but maybe Jesus is speaking of loved ones in Heaven who know when someone comes to Christ because of their life and testimony. That certainly would be a cause for celebration, wouldn't it? Imagine this for a moment: You are up in Heaven. Your daughter, your son, your grandchild, your great grandchild, an old buddy you used to work with, or someone you shared the gospel with comes to Christ. Rejoicing and applause break out. You celebrate, too, because this person is part of your life and testimony. Maybe he or she resisted your best, most faithful efforts and prayers your whole life, but now salvation has come!

Sometimes we think that it is all over when we leave this life. The applause of Heaven is there to remind us that the Lord keeps working even after we're gone (from earth).

Maybe you are only privileged to reach three people for Christ your whole life. But consider this: Those three may reach twenty. Those twenty may reach forty. Those forty may reach a hundred. When all is said and done, your testimony may end up reaching hundreds, even thousands, of people. You might even be the next Edward Kimball. One of those people who come to Christ two, three, or four generations down the road might be the next Billy Graham. The Bible describes that as "fruit that increases to your credit" (Phil. 4:17). It all comes back to your faithful witness. Could it be that in Heaven we are made aware of these things? If a party breaks out in Heaven, don't you think I will know about it? Don't you think I would want to join in the festivities?

Did you know that Noah lived 120 years and never had a single convert? He stands as an example for all the faithful "seed-sowers" out there who cannot always easily measure their success in sharing the gospel, at least *outwardly.* Missionary George Smith may have thought his ministry was a failure. He had been in Africa only a short time when he was driven from the country, leaving behind only *one* convert, a poor woman. Smith died not long after that, while on his knees praying for Africa. Years later, a group of men stumbled onto the place where George Smith had prayed. They also found a copy of the Scriptures he had left behind in Africa. Then they met the one convert of Smith's ministry. The result of the encounter of these men with the Bible and this woman was huge. One hundred years afterward, a mission agency discovered thirteen thousand people emerged from the ministry of missionary George Smith.

Faithfulness to what God has called us to do is the true measure of success.

And please note something else here. Jesus says there is joy over just "one sinner who repents." I've done a fair amount of evangelism, and this wording is good news to me! You know, sometimes when we invite people to Christ in our evangelistic outreaches, a lot will come. Sometimes the whole front of the stage is filled with people. We have seen thousands of people come forward at some crusades, spreading down through the aisles. In fact, one evening we saw five thousand people come forward at Angel Stadium in Anaheim, California, to make a profession of faith to follow Jesus Christ. It's easy for our hearts to leap on such occasions. Who *wouldn't* want to celebrate? But we need to keep in mind that it's due to the grace of God. As Paul said, "I planted, Apollos watered, but God gave the growth" (1 Cor. 3:6).

Other times, maybe only a handful of folks will respond—or only one. And that's due to the grace of God, too. Unfortunately, on such days, we can be tempted to say, "Hey, it didn't go that well today." *Really?* If that person who came forward was your mother, your husband, or your child, I think it would be a big deal to you. Trust me: It is a big deal to God, and it should be a big deal to us, however many people repent. Heaven rejoices when people come to faith, whether one or a multitude. Each one is valuable to the Lord. Each life matters.

Sometimes at church when we invite people to trust in Christ, very few will respond, and we're too disappointed to applaud. Well, applaud anyway, please! I don't know what you do here on earth when someone responds, but I know what Heaven does. There is excitement. There is rejoicing. Why? Evangelism is important to God. He cares about lost people. Yes, there is joy in the presence of the angels!

And finally Jesus presents a third story, about a father who has lost a son. Trust me, I can really relate to this one.

There was a man who had two sons. And the younger of them said to his father, "Father, give me the share of property that is coming to me." And he divided his property between them. Not many days later, the younger son gathered all he had and took a journey into a far country, and there he squandered his property in reckless living. And when he had spent everything, a severe famine arose in that country, and he began to be in need. So he went and hired himself out to one of the citizens of that country, who sent him into his fields to feed pigs. And he was longing to be fed with the pods that the pigs ate, and no one gave him anything.

But when he came to himself, he said, "How many of my father's hired servants have more than enough bread, but I perish here with hunger! I will arise and go to my father, and I will say to him, 'Father, I have sinned against heaven and before you. I am no longer worthy to be called your son. Treat me as one of your hired servants.'" And he arose and came to his father. But while he was still a long way off, his father saw him and felt compassion, and ran and embraced him and kissed him. And the son said to him, "Father, I have sinned against heaven and before you. I am no longer worthy to be called your son." But the father said to his servants, "Bring quickly the best robe, and put it on him, and put a ring on his hand, and shoes on his feet. And bring the fattened calf and kill it, and let us eat and celebrate. For this my son was dead, and is alive again; he was lost, and is found." And they began to celebrate.

Now his older son was in the field, and as he came and drew near to the house, he heard music and dancing. And he called one of the servants and asked what these things meant. And he said to him, "Your brother has come, and your father has killed the fattened calf, because he has received him back safe and sound." But he was angry and refused to go in. His father came out and entreated him, but he answered his father, "Look, these many years I have served you, and I never disobeyed your command, yet you never gave me a young goat, that I might celebrate with my friends. But when this son of yours came, who has devoured your property with prostitutes, you killed the fattened calf for him!" And he said to him, "Son, you are always with me, and all that is mine is yours. It was fitting to celebrate and be glad, for this your brother was dead, and is alive; he was lost, and is found." (Lk. 15:11-32)

In this story, one of the father's two sons is lost. Imagine if you were the father or mother of that child — and perhaps you are. Jesus is telling us that God joins the celebration when people come home. In fact, He organizes it and sends out the invitations! Do you want to be included?

A number of years ago, we did a crusade in San Jose. After our first night of preaching and ministry, we went to our hotel. As I was trying to go to sleep, all of a sudden I heard some music in the next room — really loud music. I could hear and feel the thump-thump-thump of a bass. I must say that I have never heard such loud music coming from a room. I put my hand up to the wall and could feel it vibrating. Some guys were having a bachelor party.

So I called security.

Well, let me tell you, in Heaven the partying is nonstop, because there is *always* someone coming to Jesus — and no one is going to call security!

Yes, evangelism is a Christian duty, but it is also a Christian *joy*. We need to do evangelism, support evangelism (both here and across every culture), and honor and encourage those who do the hard work of evangelism (see 2 Tim. 4:5). And when they help bring home the harvest, we ought to celebrate with them. God, the angels, and the redeemed in Heaven join in hearty celebration whenever a sinner repents. If that's the case, can you think of any reason why we shouldn't echo the chorus of heavenly praise here on earth?

And as we do, we need to keep looking up, because our Lord could come for us at any time. Are you ready?

CHAPTER 12

IN THE TWINKLING OF AN EYE

You are going about your business one day, thinking about the next task on your agenda or maybe just feeling a little bit hungry and wondering when lunch will come. Suddenly, in a moment so brief that you can't even measure it, you hear the blast of a trumpet, the sound of which penetrates to your very marrow, and you find yourself caught up in the air, reunited with loved ones and face-to-face with Jesus Himself.

We've discussed how the Lord occasionally lifts the shroud of Heaven and allows us to see through the gloom of this world and peer, however briefly, into the next dimension. In this chapter, we're going to talk about the *invasion* of Heaven. Titus 2:13 calls this event "our blessed hope, the appearing of the glory of our great God and Savior Jesus Christ."

Friend, I believe that the next event on the prophetic calendar is the Rapture. That is the moment when believers are caught up in the air to meet the Lord—in new, resurrected bodies—and reunited with loved ones who have gone before us. Are you prepared for that awesome event, which the Bible says will happen "in the twinkling of an eye"?

Mark Hitchcock, in his excellent book *Could the Rapture Happen Today?*, says: "The rapture of the church is that future event when Jesus Christ will descend from heaven to resurrect the bodies of departed believers and to transform and translate the bodies of living believers immediately into His glorious presence in a moment of time and then escort them to heaven to live with Him forever."[1]

Some critics of this teaching are skeptical because the word rapture does not appear in the Bible. Of course, if that is the standard on whether to believe a teaching, then we are going to have to throw out the doctrine of the Trinity, too, because you won't find the word Trinity in the Bible. But of course the pages of Scripture tell us much about the triune God — that this one God eternally exists as Father, Son, and Holy Spirit. Just because the Bible doesn't use our word, "Trinity," to describe this truth doesn't negate it. I would also remind you that the word Bible is not used in the Bible! But we still refer to Scripture as such. The same is true with the Rapture. While this particular word is not used in our English Bibles, it describes a reality that is clearly taught in Scripture.

The most well-known passage about the Rapture is probably this one:

We do not want you to be uninformed, brothers, about those who are asleep, that you may not grieve as others do who have no hope. For since we believe that Jesus died and rose again, even so, through Jesus, God will bring with him those who have fallen asleep. For this we declare to you by a word from the Lord, that we who are alive, who are left until the coming of the Lord, will not precede those who have fallen asleep. For the Lord himself will descend from heaven with a cry of command, with the voice of an archangel, and with the sound of the trumpet of God. And the dead in Christ will rise first. Then we who are alive, who are left, will be caught up together with them in the clouds to meet the Lord in the air, and so we will always be with the Lord. Therefore encourage one another with these words. (1 Thess. 4:13-18)

The Greek word that the English Standard Version and many others translate as "caught up" is *harpazo* (ἀρπάζω). The word harpazo is used thirteen times in the New Testament. It means to take forcibly, to snatch, or to catch up. Where, then, did we get the word rapture? The Latin Vulgate, which held sway in the Western church for centuries, translates the Greek using the verb rapio, "to catch up" or "take away" — thus, "rapture." Other words are used for the concept we call the Rapture as well.

Let's look at the context in 1 Thessalonians. The apostle Paul was talking to believers in Thessalonica. They were worried that loved ones who had already died would miss out on the coming of Christ. To calm their hysteria, Paul tells them about the Rapture. In 1 Thessalonians 4:13 he says that "we do not want you to be uninformed, brothers, about those who are asleep, that you may not grieve as others do who have no hope." Translation: "I don't want you to panic about this. I don't want you to worry. I don't want you to grieve as though there is no hope. You will see your loved ones again."

Some people say it doesn't really matter if you believe in the Rapture or if you think it is the same as the Second Coming. The fact is, it matters a lot what you believe about these things. Paul says so. That is why he told the Thessalonians that he didn't want them to be uninformed. Then in verse 18 he says, "Encourage one another with these words." What we believe about Heaven and last things is meant to encourage us here on earth, right now. The more we know about Heaven, the better we can live on earth.

Where else is the event that we call the Rapture spoken of in Scripture? The Lord Himself spoke of it with the disciples during the Upper Room Discourse.

> In my Father's house are many rooms. If it were not so, would I have told you that I go to prepare a place for you? And if I go and prepare a place for you, I will come again and will take you to myself, that where I am you may be also. (Jn. 14:2-3)

Then of course Jesus also said in His Olivet Discourse:

> Two men will be in the field; one will be taken and one left. Two women will be grinding at the mill; one will be taken and one left. Therefore, stay awake, for you do not know on what day your Lord is coming. (Mt. 24:40-42)

Now a skeptic, undeterred, might say that there is still no example in Scripture in which a person is suddenly caught up into Heaven, so we have no warrant to believe in a Rapture. That sounds plausible—until you realize that it is simply not true. We actually have quite a number of examples. One that comes to mind is Enoch. In chapter 5, I quoted Genesis 5:24: "Enoch walked with God, and he was not, for God took him."

And that's not all. In chapter 10, we looked at Hebrews 11:5, which says, "By faith Enoch was taken up so that he should not see death, and he was not found, because God had taken him. Now before he was taken he was commended as having pleased God." So Enoch is one example. He was on earth one day, he was in Heaven the next. Perhaps as he and the Lord were walking together one day, the Lord said, "Enoch, we're closer to my house than yours. Just come home with me!" However Enoch's departure came about, we know this: he did not die a natural death, the Lord "took him."

Then there is Elijah, the wonder-working prophet who did not die a natural death either. Elijah and his successor, Elisha, were walking together one day when it happened: "As they still went on and talked, behold, chariots of fire and horses of fire separated the two of them. And Elijah went up by a whirlwind into heaven" (2 K. 2:11).

Or how about the story of Philip? He preached the gospel to a man from Ethiopia. After the man was baptized, we read in Acts 8:39-40,

> And when they came up out of the water, the Spirit of the Lord carried Philip away, and the eunuch saw him no more, and went on his way rejoicing. But Philip found himself at Azotus, and as he passed through he preached the gospel to all the towns until he came to Caesarea.

By the way, the word used to describe Philip being caught away is harpazo. Philip wasn't raptured vertically in this case. He was raptured horizontally, about thirty miles away!

The Lord Himself in effect was raptured into Heaven after He died on the cross and rose again from the dead.

> When they had come together, they asked him, "Lord, will you at this time restore the kingdom to Israel?" He said to them, "It is not for you to know times or seasons that the Father has fixed by his own authority. But you will receive power when the Holy Spirit has come upon you, and you will be my witnesses in Jerusalem and in all Judea and Samaria, and to the end of the earth." And when he had said these things, as they were looking on, he was lifted up, and a cloud took him out of their sight. (Acts 1:6-9)

These scriptural examples and more demonstrate that the Rapture is a biblical doctrine. So when will it happen? The truth is, I don't know — nor does anyone else. Anyone who says otherwise is wrong. A few years ago, a broadcaster predicted the date of the return of Christ, not once but twice. He was wrong both times, and some of his followers lost their life savings renting billboard space to tell the world that the end was coming on a specific day. It was all very sad, and the man who said it later had to admit he was wrong. And so will any other person who comes along with a date, because no one knows the day or the hour of the return of Jesus Christ.

> Concerning that day and hour no one knows, not even the angels of heaven, nor the Son, but the Father only. For as were the days of Noah, so will be the coming of the Son of Man. For as in those days before the flood they were eating and drinking, marrying and giving in marriage, until the day when Noah entered the ark, and they were unaware until the flood came and swept them all away, so will be the coming of the Son of Man. (Mt. 24:36-39)

No one on earth knows the day or the hour. However, this also means the Rapture can happen at any time. As far as I am concerned, it could happen today, before you finish reading this chapter. It could happen tonight, after you have climbed into bed. It could happen tomorrow, just as you are putting the toothpaste on your brush. And it will happen so quickly that you won't be able to measure it in human time. Paul writes of this unfathomable speed in his great chapter on the Resurrection:

> Behold! I tell you a mystery. We shall not all sleep, but we shall all be changed, in a moment, in the twinkling of an eye, at the last trumpet. For the trumpet will sound, and the dead will be raised imperishable, and we shall be changed. (1 Cor. 15:51-52)

Now it has been said that the twinkling of an eye is about one-thousandth of a second. Another source says it is about one six-billionth of a second.[2] However long a twinkling is, the idea is that it is so quick, you can't even measure it. It is an indivisible unit of time. One moment you are living your life on earth; the next, you are caught up in the air to see Jesus.

But as fast as the Rapture happens, there is an order to it. Remember that Paul said that "the dead in Christ will rise first. Then we who are alive, who are left, will be caught up together with them in the clouds to meet the Lord in the air." Remember how the Thessalonians were worried about what happens to a person who dies as a Christian? Quite simply, Scripture teaches that to be absent from the body is to be present with the Lord (see 2 Cor. 5:8). Such people go straight to Heaven.

Then if they are in Heaven right now, how is it that they go up *first* in the Rapture? I believe Scripture teaches that our spirits are in Heaven with Jesus now and our bodies will be resurrected in the Rapture. Remember, "the dead will be raised imperishable." We will speak more about the Resurrection in the last chapter, but suffice it to say now that we will *all* be changed.

So what kind of body do Christians who are already in Heaven have? The short answer is, we don't know. The Bible doesn't say. Is there an intermediate body between our earthly flesh and the new, glorified body? We don't know the answer to this, either, but certainly there is no lack of ideas.

Many books have been written alleging that the authors have gone to Heaven and now will reveal what they have seen. While these may be fascinating, we must be very careful to compare all of these "revelations" to Scripture, which is the only reliable authority on the afterlife, and for that matter the "before" life! With regard to the form we will take in Heaven before the Resurrection, I think it is safe to say, with the apostle Paul, "For now we see through a glass, darkly" (1 Cor. 13:12, KJV)!

Now sometimes there is confusion between the Rapture and the Second Coming. Some people lump them together as one event. But according to Scripture, they are two separate events. Both can be described as the Lord's return, of course, but there are important differences:

- In the Rapture, He comes in the air. In the Second Coming, He returns to the earth.
- In the Rapture, He comes for His church. In the Second Coming, He returns with His church.
- In the Rapture, He comes like a thief in the night. In the Second Coming, every eye will see Him (see Rev. 1:7).
- In the Rapture, He comes before judgment. In the Second Coming, He returns with judgment.

So what comes after the Rapture, which is the next agenda item on God's end-times prophetic calendar? Well, whole books have been written on this important subject, and this is a volume on Heaven, so I will keep it brief, while encouraging you to consult with other sources, including my own book, *Signs of the Times*.[3]

The book of Revelation has some significant things to say on this topic. Keep in mind, the word Revelation means "The unveiling." It is not God's desire to conceal but to reveal. I'm going to give you the Reader's Digest version, but the last book of the Bible gives us a pretty clear road map of what's ahead. Here's how it begins:

The revelation of Jesus Christ, which God gave him to show to his

servants the things that must soon take place. He made it known by
sending his angel to his servant John, who bore witness to the word
of God and to the testimony of Jesus Christ, even to all that he saw.
Blessed is the one who reads aloud the words of this prophecy, and
blessed are those who hear, and who keep what is written in it, for the
time is near. (1:1-3)

Right off the bat we see that the book is by and about Jesus Christ,
who is the ultimate aim of prophecy. We also notice that the events the
book describes "must soon take place," or must happen in quick suc-
cession, like a bunch of dominoes falling. Finally, we are told that
those who take Revelation to heart receive a blessing. So let's see what
Revelation says about the future, and prepare to be blessed!

One of the unique things about Revelation is that it comes with its
own outline. After encountering the risen and sovereign Christ in
Revelation 1:4-18, John records this instruction from the Lord:

"Write therefore the things that you have seen, those that are and
those that are to take place after this" (1:19).

This is a three-part overview of Revelation. What John saw, in 1:4-20,
was the resurrected and glorified Jesus, with all power in Heaven and
on earth: "His eyes were like a flame of fire, his feet were like bur-
nished bronze . . . and his voice was like the roar of many waters"
(1:14-15). The things that are include the Lord's instructions to the
seven churches (2–3). The things that are to take place after this are
described in the rest of the book (4–22). What are those things? They
occur after the church has finished its work on earth—that is, after
the Rapture.

This final section of the book begins with the sound of a trumpet
in Revelation 4:1:

After this I looked, and behold, a door standing open in heaven! And
the first voice, which I had heard speaking to me like a trumpet, said,
"Come up here, and I will show you what must take place after this."

Now where have we heard about a trumpet before? Over in 1 Thessalonians 4, we read, "For the Lord himself will descend from heaven with a cry of command, with the voice of an archangel, and with the sound of the trumpet of God. And the dead in Christ will rise first." Then in 1 Corinthians 15 we read about "the last trumpet."

But be sure to notice the wording in Revelation 4:1: These things "must take place." It will all happen precisely as predicted. The future is sure, because it is in God's hands.

Let's think about John for a minute. As we have already seen, he is on the island of Patmos. Banished. Alone. Writing the words of Revelation being given by Jesus. Now look back at Revelation 3, when Jesus has just said to the church of Laodicea, "Behold, I stand at the door and knock. If anyone hears my voice and opens the door, I will come in to him and eat with him, and he with me. The one who conquers, I will grant him to sit with me on my throne, as I also conquered and sat down with my Father on his throne" (vv. 20-21). John is one of those who is conquering the world by his faith.

And as John is writing these words, suddenly a door is opened, and he is hurtled into the presence of God. Let's read about it in Revelation 4:2: "At once," John writes, "I was in the Spirit, and behold, a throne stood in heaven, with one seated on the throne." John is there in "the twinkling of an eye"! John is raptured, if you will.

This marks a major shift in Revelation. We go from a focus on the church to what is ahead. It is worth noting that the church is not mentioned in chapters 4 to 19. That's because believers are in Heaven during the Great Tribulation. This seven-year period will begin when a figure known as the Antichrist emerges. Now people will become believers after the Rapture, but all true believers up to this point are caught up to meet the Lord before the Antichrist is revealed and the Great Tribulation period begins.

At first, the situation will look promising. The Antichrist will come as a man of peace. Deluded and desperate people will see him as someone with economic solutions. A charismatic individual, the Antichrist will be loved by many. Some will think he is the Messiah. He will even help the Jews to rebuild their temple.

But at the three-and-a-half-year midpoint (see Dan. 9:27-28), the Antichrist will erect an image of himself in the temple, commanding everyone to worship it (see Rev. 13:15-16). Jesus refers to this event in Matthew 24:15 as the abomination of desolation. And then a new and terrifying phase in the Tribulation breaks out, when God's judgment is poured out upon the earth.

At this point, God raises up 144,000 people preaching the gospel (see Rev. 7:4-8; 14:1-5). Everything builds to the battle of Armageddon (see Rev. 16:14), culminating in the Valley of Megiddo in Israel. Christ returns at the Second Coming (see Revelation 19), along with those who have already gone up to meet the Lord in the Rapture. Then the Millennium, a thousand-year reign of global peace and harmony, begins on the earth (see Rev. 20:1-6). A brief rebellion is crushed (see Rev. 20:7-10), leading to the Great White Throne Judgment (see Rev. 20:11-15). And then the New Jerusalem comes down from Heaven (see Revelation 21-22). We will learn more about the meaning of these crucial events in the rest of this book.

But here is the question I want to ask you now, in light of the fact that the Rapture could happen at any instant: Are you prepared? Those who love the Lord, whether living or dead, will meet Him joyously in the air. Those who don't will face tribulation and judgment. The bottom line is that Heaven is not the default destination of every person. You don't automatically go to Heaven when you die, no matter what the guardians of pop culture may say. As we saw in the story of the rich man and Lazarus, one went to torment. The other went to comfort. Their fate concerning Heaven was decided by what happened on earth.

The fact is, what we do on earth has repercussions in eternity. Don't get tangled up in questions of predestination and free will. From an earthly perspective, *you* decide where you will go. *You* decide if you will go to Heaven. *You* decide if you will go to Hell. But God doesn't want you to go to Hell (see 2 Pet. 3:9). He wants you to join Him in Heaven. But you must respond to His offer of forgiveness, which was purchased for you by Christ on the cross. If you will turn from your sin and put your faith in Jesus, you can know with confidence that you will go to Heaven when you die. If the Rapture happens before that, and it could, you can be confident that you will be ready to meet Him.

We all have an appointment with God, when life on this earth as we know it will end and we will enter eternity. You may think that you know when that day is, but you don't. No one knows the day or the hour. Only God does. So you must be ready. Are you?

Does the prospect of the Lord Jesus coming suddenly and unexpectedly thrill you or scare you? Remember that Jesus said, "One will be taken and the other will be left." Some people will be caught up to meet the Lord and others will be left on this earth. Who will be taken? Believers in Jesus. Who will be left? People who don't believe in Jesus. It is as simple as that. If you want that door open for you in Heaven, you have to open the door in your heart. So get right with God or you will get left. This is not a fairy tale. It is true. It is the gospel.

CHAPTER 13

HERE COMES THE JUDGE

ometimes people say that the problem with humanity is our environment. If only we could give kids good parents, or decent housing, or
a good education, or healthy food, or recreational opportunities, or self-
esteem, we could get rid of crime, selfishness, risky behaviors, and
poverty. Man's basic problem, they assert with perfect confidence, is not
a bad heart. It is a bad environment. It's not *who* we are; it's *where* we are.

Such people, well-meaning though they are, obviously have not
read Revelation 20. Or at least they have not understood it. This next-
to-next-to-last chapter in the Bible describes both a paradise gained
and a paradise lost. It is the story of people learning about human sin
and God's law the hard way.

In the previous chapter, we looked at the Rapture—the sudden,
unknown day when Christ comes for His church. In this one we will
look at the millennial reign of Christ, or Millennium for short. The
Millennium, of course, will last for a thousand years and will come after
the Great Tribulation, the battle of Armageddon, and the Second
Coming, when our Lord will return and put evil to flight. At this point
chronologically in God's prophetic calendar, Heaven has come to earth
and the prayer of Christ—for God's will to be done on earth as it is in
Heaven—will be answered. The saints will be ruling and reigning with
the Lord.

Even better, the Devil will be chained in the bottomless pit for a
thousand years. He won't be able to tempt anyone. He won't be able to
harass anyone. He won't be able to accuse anyone. So the Millennium

will be the epitome of the good environment.

> I saw an angel coming down from heaven, holding in his hand the key to the bottomless pit and a great chain. And he seized the dragon, that ancient serpent, who is the devil and Satan, and bound him for a thousand years, and threw him into the pit, and shut it and sealed it over him, so that he might not deceive the nations any longer, until the thousand years were ended. After that he must be released for a little while. (Rev. 20:1-3)

What is the world going to be like when the Lord comes back and rules in the Millennium?

1. There is finally going to be world peace. Whatever might be in the offing now concerning nations such as North Korea or Iran, we know this much: When Christ comes back again, war will end. Isaiah 2:4 says,

> He shall judge between the nations,
>   and shall decide disputes for many peoples;
> and they shall beat their swords into plowshares,
>   and their spears into pruning hooks;
> nation shall not lift up sword against nation,
>   neither shall they learn war anymore.

Not for nothing is Jesus Christ called the Prince of Peace (see Is. 9:6). One day He will bring not only peace in our hearts, but peace in our world.

2. In the millennial reign of Christ, we will experience some things but not others. We *will* have joy and happiness. We will *not have* disabilities, depression, wheelchairs, walkers, blindness, or deafness. Isaiah 35:5-6 says,

Then the eyes of the blind shall be opened,
 and the ears of the deaf unstopped;
then shall the lame man leap like a deer,
 and the tongue of the mute sing for joy.

3. Mortals who survive the Tribulation will live long human lives. Those believers who return with Christ will live forever. Isaiah 65:20 says,

No more shall there be in it
 an infant who lives but a few days,
 or an old man who does not fill out his days,
for the young man shall die a hundred years old,
 and the sinner a hundred years old shall be accursed.

Maybe life expectancies will be extended into the hundreds of years, as they were in Genesis.

4. The animal kingdom will be subdued. Isaiah 11:6 says,

The wolf shall dwell with the lamb,
 and the leopard shall lie down with the young goat,
and the calf and the lion and the fattened calf together;
 and a little child shall lead them.

5. There will be universal justice and righteousness. No more corrupt lawyers. No more activist judges. No more frivolous lawsuits. No more criminals going free. Psalm 72:2,4 says,

May he judge your people with righteousness,
 and your poor with justice! . . .
May he defend the cause of the poor of the people,
 give deliverance to the children of the needy,
 and crush the oppressor!

6. Holiness will prevail. All the world will be filled with the knowledge of the Lord. Isaiah 35:8 says,

> A highway shall be there,
>   and it shall be called the Way of Holiness;
> the unclean shall not pass over it.
>   It shall belong to those who walk on the way;
>   even if they are fools, they shall not go astray.

Despite all these blessings in the Millennium, amazingly, there is going to be a rebellion of mankind against God. You say, "How is that even possible? Why would we rebel against God?" The good news is, the believers who have met the Lord in the air and returned with Him to reign on the earth won't be in the rebellion. We will be in glorified bodies and will be temptation-proof and sin-proof. But the regular mortals on the earth at this time who have survived the Tribulation will be there. They will still have sin natures. They will have children, and their children will have children. Fast forward a thousand years. There will be a final rebellion of mankind against God, and then judgment.

> I saw thrones, and seated on them were those to whom the authority to judge was committed. Also I saw the souls of those who had been beheaded for the testimony of Jesus and for the word of God, and those who had not worshiped the beast or its image and had not received its mark on their foreheads or their hands. They came to life and reigned with Christ for a thousand years. The rest of the dead did not come to life until the thousand years were ended. This is the first resurrection. Blessed and holy is the one who shares in the first resurrection! Over such the second death has no power, but they will be priests of God and of Christ, and they will reign with him for a thousand years.
>
> And when the thousand years are ended, Satan will be released from his prison and will come out to deceive the nations that are at the four corners of the earth, Gog and Magog, to gather them for

battle; their number is like the sand of the sea. And they marched up over the broad plain of the earth and surrounded the camp of the saints and the beloved city, but fire came down from heaven and consumed them, and the devil who had deceived them was thrown into the lake of fire and sulfur where the beast and the false prophet were, and they will be tormented day and night forever and ever. (Rev. 20:4-10)

See how dark the human heart is! The key to human sin and failure is not outside us; it is inside us! You couldn't have a better, more prosperous, more peaceful, more just time on earth than the Millennium. This is literally the closest that you will be able to get to Heaven while on earth. Christ Himself will be running the show. We will be ruling and reigning with the Lord. Righteousness will fill the planet. Still there will be rebellion. Why? Because the heart of man is wicked.

How wicked? Sometimes people will justify their actions and say, "Well, God knows my heart," as if that knowledge will somehow clear them. But the heart is precisely the problem. God knows your heart. Your heart is "deceitful above all things, and desperately sick," according to Jeremiah 17:9. Ecclesiastes 9:3 says that "the hearts of the children of man are full of evil, and madness is in their hearts while they live."

We wonder how a rebellion could occur at a time like this, but we forget that this won't even be the first time such a thing has happened. The first rebellion against God occurred, of all places, in Heaven. Satan, after all, wasn't always the Devil. At some point, he turned against God, and a third of the angels followed him in his rebellion (see Rev. 12:4). And, of course, Adam and Eve rebelled against God in the Garden of Eden (see Genesis 3). A good environment is no barrier to evil!

This dynamic happens even in our homes. We raise our children in the way of the Lord. We teach them the Bible. We do everything we know to do. Then they rebel. We think, "I am a failure as a parent." Listen, if having a prodigal means that we are failures, then who is a bigger failure as a Parent than our heavenly Father? God has a lot of prodigals, doesn't He? No, having a prodigal proves nothing about whether you were a good mother or father.

So at the end of the Millennium, the Devil will not have changed during his time of incarceration. Like a hardened criminal who is released only to commit more crimes, the Devil will effectively pick up where he left off. He will, like the dog returning to its vomit (see Prov. 26:11), shake his fist at God one final time, seeking to take as many people as possible with him. His doom is sobering: "The devil who had deceived them was thrown into the lake of fire and sulfur where the beast and the false prophet were, and they will be tormented day and night forever and ever" (Rev. 20:10).

Now we come to the subject of this chapter, the Great White Throne Judgment. It is the final judgment, not of the Devil, but of mankind.

> I saw a great white throne and him who was seated on it. From his presence earth and sky fled away, and no place was found for them. And I saw the dead, great and small, standing before the throne, and books were opened. Then another book was opened, which is the book of life. And the dead were judged by what was written in the books, according to what they had done. And the sea gave up the dead who were in it, Death and Hades gave up the dead who were in them, and they were judged, each one of them, according to what they had done. Then Death and Hades were thrown into the lake of fire. This is the second death, the lake of fire. And if anyone's name was not found written in the book of life, he was thrown into the lake of fire. (20:11-15)

Read it again . . . slowly . . . out loud. Reflect on it. Picture your-self there when the earth and the sky flee away, the ground opens up wide, and the only thing you can see is the Judge with a gaze you cannot bear. People are rightly concerned about a government that can go through all their telephone calls and online activity. We all demand privacy in the world. But before the Great White Throne there will be no privacy. The books will be opened, and everything about your life will be known. Does that frighten you? It should! Every evil, thought-less venality you have ever committed will be emblazoned across the sky for all to see. Every opportunity to do the good that you ignored will be on display, like a celestial billboard. All the people you treated shabbily, or laughed at, or ignored will be witnesses against you.

Your evil heart will be on display. You will be guilty — "without," as the old hymn says, "one plea."

Lost people sometimes joke about how they will party when they get to Hell. Friend, I can assure you, there will be no partying in Hell, not even by the Devil. This is perhaps the most tragic passage in all of the Bible. No wonder the sign at the entrance to Dante's *Inferno* says, "Abandon hope, all ye who enter here." The Great White Throne is the final court. There are no appeals of its judgments. There will be no debate over anyone's guilt or innocence. There will be a prosecutor, but no defender. There will be an accuser, but no advocate. There will be an indictment, but no defense. There will be convicting evidence, but no rebuttal or cross examination. There will be a Judge, but no jury. That Judge's holy verdict is final and binding for all eternity.

When a nonbeliever dies, he goes to Hades, also known as Hell. What is that place like? In an earlier chapter about Luke 16, we saw that the sinner was "in torment" in Hades. By the way, the word tor-ment is used four times in that text. People in Hades are fully con-scious and in tormenting pain. There is no reincarnation or purgatory. Nonbelievers who die go to Hades. According to the Bible, physical death is a separation of the soul from the body. It constitutes a transi-tion from the visible world to the invisible. For the believer, it marks the entrance into the presence of God. For the nonbeliever, it is their entrance to Hades. This is the first death.

But we are looking in this chapter at the Great White Throne Judgment, when Hades is emptied of its occupants. Those who stand at the Great White Throne Judgment have been sent from jail (Hades) to face the final verdict of the Judge before being sent to their eternal prison. That prison is as horrible as it is inescapable — the lake of fire. This is the second death. If you end up in this place, it is too late. No one will have to tell you to abandon all hope. You will know.

Question: Who will be at the White Throne Judgment? Answer: Everyone who has rejected God's offer of forgiveness through Jesus Christ. Most of us like the sound of Jesus' words in John 3:16-17:

> God so loved the world, that he gave his only Son, that whoever believes in him should not perish but have eternal life. For God did not send his Son into the world to condemn the world, but in order that the world might be saved through him.

But John 3:18 lays out absolute parameters about who will be saved — and who won't be:

> Whoever believes in him is not condemned, but whoever does not believe is condemned already, because he has not believed in the name of the only Son of God.

"Whoever does not believe is condemned already." As I have said before, Heaven is not the default setting for every person. We are bound for Hell unless we trust in Christ and in His gracious work on the cross. Those who will stand condemned at the Great White Throne Judgment are all those sinners who would not open their hearts to Jesus Christ.

They will be out-and-out sinners. I like to call them garden variety sinners. They are sinners and proud of it. They live their lives. They shake their fists at God. They go out of their way to "do it their way." They break the commandments. They don't care. In fact, they like to break commandments. These are the folks who have lived godless lives. They will be there at the Great White Throne Judgment.

But self-righteous people will be there, too. They are a little different from the garden variety sinners. Self-righteous people are kind people. They are considerate people. They don't think they need forgiveness. Maybe they volunteer and help out. They do benevolent things. We all know people like this. They may say, "I live by the Ten

Commandments," even though they probably couldn't name them all if you spotted them five. But even if they could, please remember: We don't get to Heaven based on our goodness. Heaven is not for perfect people. It is for forgiven people. Titus 3:5 says that "he saved us, not because of works done by us in righteousness, but according to his own mercy."

The procrastinators will be there, too. Procrastinators are the ones who put it off. They might say, "I accept in premise what you say. I believe that the Bible is true. I believe Jesus Christ is the way to God. One of these days, I am going to get right with God. One of these days, I am going to go to church. One of these days, I am going to make changes. But not today." They will be there.

Unsaved church members will be there, too. They have their Bibles. They sing our songs. They pray with us. They know all about God. But they don't know God. These people can expect the following pro-nouncement from Jesus:

> Not everyone who says to me, "Lord, Lord," will enter the kingdom of heaven, but the one who does the will of my Father who is in heaven. On that day many will say to me, "Lord, Lord, did we not prophesy in your name, and cast out demons in your name, and do many mighty works in your name?" And then will I declare to them, "I never knew you; depart from me, you workers of lawlessness." (Mt. 7:21-23)

What "lawless" deeds did they do? They prophesied in His name. They cast out demons in His name. Aren't those good things? Yes, but they are not *saving* things. If you are a Christian, good works will char-acterize your life, but those works won't save you. Salvation is "not because of works done . . . in righteousness." Maybe some will say, "Did we not receive communion in your name?" "Did we not get bap-tized in your name?" "Did we not give a confession in your name?" But He will say, "Depart from me." It is a sobering scene. As the apos-tle Paul said, "Examine yourselves, to see whether you are in the faith.

Test yourselves" (2 Cor. 13:5). You don't want to be wrong.

So we know *who* will be there at the Great White Throne Judgment. I pray to God that you will not be in that tragic throng. *What* will happen there? Revelation 20:12 describes the scene.

> I saw the dead, great and small, standing before the throne, and books were opened. Then another book was opened, which is the book of life. And the dead were judged by what was written in the books, according to what they had done.

Unlike us, God is no respecter of persons. He doesn't care if someone was a king, a queen, a prime minister, a president, a billionaire, a rock star, an actor . . . or a ditch-digger. Everyone, great and small, will stand before the Judge in awful, clarifying equality. As we have seen, John 3:18 says, "Whoever believes in him is not condemned, but whoever does not believe is condemned already, because he has not believed in the name of the only Son of God."

Another question: If the nonbeliever is already condemned, why is the Last Judgment even needed? Why not simply get on with it? Answer: The purpose of this final confrontation between God and man is to clearly demonstrate to the nonbeliever why he or she is already condemned. At the Judgment, "books" and a "book" will be opened. The "book" is the Book of Life—more on that later. But what are in the "books"? We are not told, but we can speculate, drawing from other passages of Scripture.

Maybe one of these books is the book of God's commandments. Why did God give us the commandments? The commandments were given not to make us righteous—we have evil, unbelieving hearts, remember?—but to show us we can never be righteous. In fact, we are told in Romans 3:19, "Now we know that whatever the law says it speaks to those who are under the law, so that every mouth may be stopped, and the whole world may be held accountable to God." The law opens our eyes and closes our mouths. I look at God's standards and realize I am a sinner, garden variety or otherwise.

Another book might be a record of everything we have ever said or done. I am told in Ecclesiastes 12:14, "For God will bring every deed into judgment, with every secret thing, whether good or evil." That is kind of scary, isn't it? Everything you have said and done. Every conversation. Every phone call. Every e-mail. Every text. It is all recorded — and by a Judge far holier and more powerful than any government agency.

Maybe another of these books will note the fact that people did not even live by their own standards. Some folks will say, "I don't really believe in organized religion. I have my own belief system. I have my own values." My experience tells me that most of the people who say this are simply dodging the issue: the necessity of following Jesus Christ. But let's give them the benefit of the doubt and say they are indeed trying to follow a moral code of their own devising. The fact is, however, Romans 2:14 says that even when we say we follow our own law, we know enough of God's law to stand guilty before Him.

I think another of these books might be a record of every time you have heard the gospel. While there are certainly millions of people in true spiritual darkness — never having heard the plan of salvation — in the Buddhist, Hindu, Muslim, and animist worlds, the fact is, most of us have heard the gospel . . . many times. For us, I expect the Lord is keeping a record of every time we heard the gospel from our earliest days. Maybe, like D. L. Moody, you heard it in Sunday school. Maybe, like Billy Graham, you heard it at a crusade. What did you do with it? The Bible says we will be judged according to the light we had (see Mt. 11:21-24; Lk. 12:48).

Now here is another question: If God is all loving, why did He even invent Hell? Heaven, at least in part, was invented for good people. However, Hell was invented, if you will, for the Devil and his angels. God did not design Hell for people, but for the Devil.

Do you think the Devil deserves to go to Hell? As terrible as Hell is, of course he does. For justice to prevail, the punishment must fit the crime. Hell is certainly an appropriate punishment for the father of lies, don't you think? How about all those demons that followed him?

Do they deserve Hell? Again, yes. What about people? Do they deserve Hell, too? Well, if people, through their own anti-God habits, dispositions, and choices go the Devil's way, doesn't it stand to reason that they will end up with the Devil? It is not so much that God sends them to Hell (although in another sense He certainly does, giving them what they want), as they go there voluntarily, following a path they have already chosen.

J. I. Packer says, "Scripture sees Hell as self-chosen. . . . [H]ell appears as God's gesture of respect for human choice. All receive what they actually chose, either to be with God forever, worshipping Him, or without God, worshipping themselves."[1] In *The Great Divorce*, C. S. Lewis wrote, "There are only two kinds of people in the end: those who say to God, 'Thy will be done,' and those to whom God says, in the end, 'Thy will be done.'"[2] All who are in Hell chose to be there.

Is there someone you are thinking of right now with whom you need to have that conversation about Jesus? My mom was a notorious prodigal for years and years. Married and divorced many times, a heavy smoker and drinker, by the time she had reached seventy, her health had broken down. I had shared the gospel with her many times, but she had never really made that solid, clear commitment to Christ.

One day I woke up and I said to Cathe, "I need to go talk to my mom today." She said, "Why?" I replied, "I just really sense the Lord is telling me to go talk to her. It is time for that conversation."

I went over to Mom's house and said, "Mom, I want to talk to you about your relationship with God."

"I don't want to talk about it." That is what she always said. My mom was stubborn. But her son was even more stubborn that day.

"We are going to talk about it today." It was not easy. It was awkward, but I pressed ahead.

I said, "I am concerned about your soul. I want to know that you will go to Heaven when you die."

We talked about these matters, and by God's grace my mom eventually made a commitment to follow Jesus Christ. What a thrill! A month later, she died. What a shock! I thought she would live for many more years. She didn't. I'm glad I had that conversation.

Listen, when God leads you to have that conversation with someone, please do it. Yes, it is awkward. Yes, it is uncomfortable. Who cares? Have it anyway. I am not trying to lay a guilt trip on you and say it is all dependent upon you and God can't work in a person's life if you don't step up to the plate. But it is an undeniable fact that God reaches people through people. So be that person. Let Him use you.

The Bible teaches that there are two deaths. One is physical. The other is spiritual. Jesus warned, "And do not fear those who kill the body but cannot kill the soul. Rather fear him who can destroy both soul and body in hell" (Mt. 10:28). We are to fear the second death more than the first. The second death is sealed at the Great White Throne Judgment. Revelation 20:14 says, "Then Death and Hades were thrown into the lake of fire. This is the second death, the lake of fire." The second death is also described in Revelation 21:8: "But as for the cowardly, the faithless, the detestable, as for murderers, the sexually immoral, sorcerers, idolaters, and all liars, their portion will be in the lake that burns with fire and sulfur, which is the second death."

The second death is eternal separation from God. Puritan pastor Thomas Watson once said, "Eternity to the godly is a day that has no sunset; eternity to the wicked is a night that has no sunrise."[3] You don't want to go into that endless night. Everyone must face God, either as their Savior or Judge. Everyone will live somewhere forever, either in eternal day or eternal night. The choice, my friend, is yours.

Those who choose to receive Christ as Savior not only get to escape the awful Great White Throne Judgment. Incredibly, they will go to Heaven and even receive rewards for their faithful service to Him. Let's take a look at this gloriously encouraging truth in our next-to-last chapter.

CHAPTER 14

HEAVEN'S REWARDS

Back in 1970, I was praying that Jesus Christ would come back. Aren't you glad that God didn't answer my prayer right then? There's probably a good chance that you or someone you love very much has come to Christ since 1970. And the size of the global church has exploded in the intervening decades. There are millions more Christians in Asia, Africa, and Latin America than there were back then, and they are doing amazing work for the kingdom.[1] If Jesus had come back when I asked Him to, they wouldn't be.

I believe the Lord is delaying because He is waiting for that one last person. Romans 11:25 speaks about the Jewish people being hardened in their response to Christ "until the fullness of the Gentiles has come in." I believe that somewhere on this planet there walks a man or a woman who is the last one. The moment he or she believes, we will be out of here, caught up to meet the Lord in the air. But we must be patient.

As 2 Peter 3:9 reminds us, "The Lord is not slow to fulfill his promise as some count slowness, but is patient toward you, not wishing that any should perish, but that all should reach repentance." Then Peter says this:

> Since all these things are thus to be dissolved, what sort of people ought you to be in lives of holiness and godliness, waiting for and hastening the coming of the day of God, because of which the heavens will be set on fire and dissolved, and the heavenly bodies will melt as they burn! (3:11-12)

Peter's point: Jesus' future coming should impact the way we live now. Remember, we are talking about the connection between life on earth and life in Heaven. I like to say there is a thin veil between these two dimensions, and one really does affect the other. A desire for Heaven ought to motivate what we do on earth.

The Lord wants us to live for Him, of course, so that we can get to Heaven by His grace. But once we have decided to follow Him and Heaven is assured, what then? Can we just put our lives in cruise control as we wait for the end? Of course not! No wonder the apostle Paul says, "Therefore, my beloved brothers, be steadfast, immovable, always abounding in the work of the Lord, knowing that in the Lord your labor is not in vain" (1 Cor. 15:58).

We not only get to escape Hell by His mercy, but we get to experience Heaven by His grace. But even more incredibly, and purely by that same grace, the Lord offers to reward us in Heaven for our faithful service on earth. We all love rewards for a job well done. The best Olympic sprinter gets a gold medal (and maybe some lucrative endorsement deals!). A hard-working mom maybe gets a day at the spa on Mother's Day. A dad might squeeze in an occasional round of golf. A hard-working employee might get a raise *and* a promotion. A *just* reward fits the actions or services rendered. Most of us are well-acquainted with the concept of rewards, and you'll be glad to know that they don't stop once we get to Heaven!

When we get to Heaven, there will finally be justice. God's justice means that He will *reward* His saints, who are saved by grace, for all their labors. As Hebrews 6:10 reminds us, "For God is not unjust so as to overlook your work and the love that you have shown for his name in serving the saints, as you still do."

It was Jesus, after all, who said, "And whoever gives one of these little ones even a cup of cold water because he is a disciple, truly, I say to you, he will by no means lose his reward" (Mt. 10:42). Think about what this means. Every time you as a follower of Christ give a child a cup of water in the name of the Lord, or help a little old lady cross the street, or write that check to the local homeless shelter or to global missions, or adopt a child, or visit someone in the hospital or nursing home, or give up your Sunday to watch a neighbor's child, or share the gospel, or engage in any one of an infinite number of opportunities to serve God and your fellow man, an entry is being made in your account book in Heaven. And one day the books will be opened.

> When the Son of Man comes in his glory, and all the angels with him, then he will sit on his glorious throne. Before him will be gathered all the nations, and he will separate people one from another as a shepherd separates the sheep from the goats. And he will place the sheep on his right, but the goats on the left. Then the King will say to those on his right, "Come, you who are blessed by my Father, inherit the kingdom prepared for you from the foundation of the world. For I was hungry and you gave me food, I was thirsty and you gave me drink, I was a stranger and you welcomed me, I was naked and you clothed me, I was sick and you visited me, I was in prison and you came to me." Then the righteous will answer him, saying, "Lord, when did we see you hungry and feed you, or thirsty and give you drink? And when did we see you a stranger and welcome you, or naked and clothe you? And when did we see you sick or in prison and visit you?" And the King will answer them, "Truly, I say to you, as you did it to one of the least of these my brothers, you did it to me." (25:31-40)

It is interesting to note here that the Lord's sheep will be surprised by all that they did. The Lord will keep track of our good deeds, so we don't have to. We are to do our good works in secret — "Beware of practicing your righteousness before other people in order to be seen by them, for then you will have no reward from your Father who is in heaven" (6:1) — and "not let your left hand know what your right hand is doing" (6:3).

As we have already seen, doing good deeds is not a competitive sport. In Heaven we won't ever say, "My crown has more stars than yours," or, "My mansion is bigger." There is no boasting in Heaven — at least about *ourselves*! God doesn't need us and doesn't owe us a thing.

"Or who has given a gift to him that he might be repaid?" (Ro. 11:35). The point is not to keep score, either with ourselves or with others. The point is to love God and our fellow man and leave the rewards to Him. As Jesus told His disciples, "So you also, when you have done all that you were commanded, say, 'We are unworthy servants; we have only done what was our duty'" (Lk. 17:10).

And yet, God still uses and rewards us! Reflecting on Jesus' words in the Sermon on the Mount about the impossibility of serving both God and money, Randy Alcorn says, "Jesus invites us to choose our treasury. Will we invest our treasures on earth and lose them when we die? Or will we invest our treasures in heaven, where they will be ours for eternity?"[2] Let's look at several passages that speak about the rewards of God — not so that we will selfishly seek them — but so that we will passionately seek Him.

In 1 Corinthians 3, Paul tells believers who are overly concerned about which celebrity church leaders they follow that Jesus Christ is the Leader who counts.

> What then is Apollos? What is Paul? Servants through whom you believed, as the Lord assigned to each. I planted, Apollos watered, but God gave the growth. So neither he who plants nor he who waters is anything, but only God who gives the growth. He who plants and he who waters are one, and each will receive his wages according to his labor. For we are God's fellow workers. You are God's field, God's building.
>
> According to the grace of God given to me, like a skilled master builder I laid a foundation, and someone else is building upon it. Let each one take care how he builds upon it. For no one can lay a foundation other than that which is laid, which is Jesus Christ. Now if anyone builds on the foundation with gold, silver, precious stones, wood, hay, straw — each one's work will become manifest, for the Day will disclose it, because it will be revealed by fire, and the fire will test what sort of work each one has done. If the work that anyone has built on the foundation survives, he will receive a reward. If

anyone's work is burned up, he will suffer loss, though he himself will be saved, but only as through fire. (vv. 5-15)

Paul says that any work done on the foundation, Jesus Christ, will not only survive, but be *rewarded*. Any work that is done for selfish motives will be burned up. Attitude is so important. We shouldn't expect a reward if our heart is rotten, even if we "do all the right things." So as we work, let's keep in mind that *God* is our ultimate reward. If we were to receive no other rewards, *He* would be enough.

The patriarch Abram (later, Abraham) had staked his whole life on the Lord. He had left Ur with Sarai (later, Sarah) for a land the Lord would show them. They lived in tents as they awaited a better country. Though promised they would become a great nation, they were childless . . . for a long time.

"Fear not, Abram," the Lord told His servant. "I am your shield; your reward shall be very great" (Gen. 15:1). The Lord reminds His servant, in the midst of very uncertain earthly circumstances, that He will protect and provide for him. Our heavenly rewards have meaning and can be counted on only because they come from the Lord our shield, who will "freely give us all things" (Ro. 8:32, NASB).

So what might these "very great" rewards from the gracious hand of our God look like? Well, we have already talked about the crowns awaiting us. They will be visible recognitions of our faith and work on the earth, suggesting our role in ruling with Him over the universe (see 2 Tim. 2:12). And though the Lord for now has made us "a little lower than the heavenly beings" (Ps. 8:5), one day "we will judge angels" (1 Cor. 6:3, NASB).

We get a foretaste of our heavenly responsibilities in the parable of the ten minas.

[Jesus] said therefore, "A nobleman went into a far country to receive for himself a kingdom and then return. Calling ten of his servants, he gave them ten minas, and said to them, 'Engage in business until I come.' But his citizens hated him and sent a delegation after him, saying, 'We do not want this man to reign over us.' When he returned, having received the kingdom, he ordered these servants to whom he had given the money to be called to him, that he might know what they had gained by doing business. The first came before him, saying, 'Lord, your mina has made ten minas more.' And he said to him, 'Well done, good servant! Because you have been faithful in a very little, you shall have authority over ten cities.' And the second came, saying, 'Lord, your mina has made five minas.' And he said to him, 'And you are to be over five cities.' Then another came, saying, 'Lord, here is your mina, which I kept laid away in a handkerchief; for I was afraid of you, because you are a severe man. You take what you did not deposit, and reap what you did not sow.' He said to him, 'I will condemn you with your own words, you wicked servant! You knew that I was a severe man, taking what I did not deposit and reaping what I did not sow? Why then did you not put my money in the bank, and at my coming I might have collected it with interest?' And he said to those who stood by, 'Take the mina from him, and give it to the one who has the ten minas.' And they said to him, 'Lord, he has ten minas!' 'I tell you that to everyone who has, more will be given, but from the one who has not, even what he has will be taken away.'" (Lk. 19:12-26)

The parable seems to suggest that we will have heavenly responsibilities commensurate with our earthly faithfulness. Indeed, it appears that we will have responsibility over "cities." What does this mean? It seems to suggest a continuing role for culture, work, development, and heavenly history.

We'll discuss these concepts more in the last chapter, but it seems clear that part of God's reward to us is a proportional gift of responsibility in administering His new Creation. Work, therefore, is not a punishment, but a gift, one we begin here but continue there. Yes, we will indeed rest in Heaven, but we will also work . . . and it will be fulfilling, energizing, exciting, and satisfying work. There will be no more working "by sweat of our brows" in Heaven!

We can point to and prepare for that heavenly work by how we approach our earthly tasks, because we work for the same reward-giving Lord in both places (see Col. 3:24). Alcorn says, "For just as God called Adam and Eve, God calls us to develop a Christ-pleasing culture and to rule the world to his glory."[3] In other words, we are to do His will on earth "as it is in Heaven." That puts our work down here in an eternal light, doesn't it?

George Allen, the late professional football coach, used to say, "The future is now." He had an older team whose objective was to win right away, not wait until an indeterminate time in the future. In a sense, this is what Christians are to do, and what we are exploring in this book. For Christians, the heavenly future begins now, while we are living on this earth. We're not so heavenly minded that we're no earthly good; we're so heavenly minded that we're a ton of earthly good.

As we live into the heavenly future right now, we need to see how a focus on Christ's rewards helps us. In Luke 12, Jesus tells us how we are to live and what we are to do in light of His imminent return with rewards.

Stay dressed for action and keep your lamps burning, and be like men who are waiting for their master to come home from the wedding feast, so that they may open the door to him at once when he comes and knocks. Blessed are those servants whom the master finds awake when he comes. Truly, I say to you, he will dress himself for service and have them recline at table, and he will come and serve them. If he comes in the second watch, or in the third, and finds them awake, blessed are those servants! But know this, that if the master of the house had known at what hour the thief was coming, he would not have left his house to be broken into. You also must be ready, for the Son of Man is coming at an hour you do not expect.

Peter said, "Lord, are you telling this parable for us or for all?" And the Lord said, "Who then is the faithful and wise manager, whom his master will set over his household, to give them their portion of food at the proper time? Blessed is that servant whom his master will find so doing when he comes. Truly, I say to you, he will set him over all his possessions." (vv. 35-44)

In Matthew 25:1-12, Jesus describes the outlines of a first-century Jewish wedding. In contrast to today's weddings, these ancient ceremonies would last for days on end. Then a reception would follow. The marriage ceremony and festivities could fill a whole week or more. And every marriage started with a mystery: When would the bridegroom come? The bride is there. The bridesmaids are on hand. The groomsmen are milling about or eating some of the goodies. All of the friends and family are waiting for the bridegroom to show up.

Finally, whether at three o'clock in the afternoon or three o'clock in the morning, an announcement rings out: "The groom is coming! The bridegroom is here!" Immediately the wedding takes place. Only those who are ready get to enjoy the feast. The idea is that we have to be ready at all times. And the Master's servants must be ready for His sudden arrival.

So how should we live as believers in the last days here on earth so that we can be ready when the Master returns? According to Luke 12:

1. We should be shining lights in a dark place. "Stay dressed for action and keep your lamps burning" (v. 35). Back in the first century, people wore long, flowing robes, with a belt cinched around the waist. When you wanted freedom of movement, you would pull your robe above your knees and tighten your belt. Dressed like this, you could answer the door quickly. You could move quickly. Keeping your lamps burning meant having sufficient oil in them. It was like having fresh batteries in your flashlight or having your phone charged. We are to be alert, mobile, and prepared. Here is the idea Jesus is communicating: Have your walking shoes on and be ready to bolt.

2. We are to be watching for Him. "Blessed are those servants

whom the master finds awake when he comes" (v. 37). As Jesus also said, "So when all these things begin to happen, stand and look up, for your salvation is near!" (21:28, NLT).

3. We should be *expectantly* awaiting His return. Luke 12:36 says, "so that they may open the door to him *at once* when he comes and knocks" (emphasis added). Are you not just ready, not just waiting, but *eager* for the Lord's return?

4. We should be *working*. Look at 12:43: "Blessed is that servant whom his master will find so doing when he comes." He is *doing* something. If watching is the evidence of faith, working is the evidence of faith in action. Watching for the Lord's return will help us prepare our own lives, but working will assure that we bring others with us. Notice that Jesus is saying there is a blessedness in living this way. Another way to translate it: "Happy are those servants whom the Master when He comes will find so watching." *Happy* are those servants. Looking for the return of the Lord is a happy, joyful, purposeful way to live.

C. H. Spurgeon once said, "It is a very blessed thing to be on the watch for Christ, it is a blessing to us now. How it detaches you from the world. You can be poor without murmuring. You can be rich without worldliness. You can be sick without sorrowing. You can be healthy without presumption. If you are always waiting for Christ's coming, untold blessings are wrapped up in that glorious hope."[4]

And yet there are more blessings still. Look at Luke 12:44: "Truly, I say to you, he will set him over all his possessions." As we have already seen, one of the rewards of faithful Christian service on earth is more work and responsibility in Heaven. This is so because things actually happen in Heaven, though we're not quite sure how. We can only speculate about what our responsibilities will be, but you can rest assured that we won't be sitting around on clouds, strumming harps and being bored!

"Behold, I am coming soon," the Lord says, "bringing my recompense with me, to repay each one for what he has done" (Rev. 22:12). The question is, will you be ready when the Lord comes with His awesome rewards?

And now we turn to the final chapter of this book about Heaven, the beginning of eternity.

CHAPTER 15

CHRIST'S RESURRECTION — AND OURS

When I was a kid, we used to go out to a little cabin in the Yucca Valley desert to spend time with my grandparents, who were from Arkansas. There was no electricity. We had to use kerosene lamps at night. We even had an outhouse. It was primitive by today's standards, but it was our special place, despite the drawbacks.

My grandmother, Mama Stella, was a great Southern cook who made everything from scratch — and I mean *scratch*! My grandfather would kill a chicken by chopping its head off on a block, with the blood spurting everywhere. But whatever trauma I experienced by seeing that grisly scene was more than compensated for by my grandmother's fried chicken. The sound of it sizzling in the pan, the thick aroma wafting from the kitchen, the crisp saltiness of the skin, and the tender juiciness of the meat inside — all these memories from our good times in Yucca Valley come flooding back and make me start salivating even today.

I won't bore you by describing her black-eyed peas, collard greens, and the best mashed potatoes I have ever had. But Mama Stella's crowning achievement was a biscuit that I have never seen equaled anywhere. In my mind, I'm *there*.

What's *your* Yucca Valley? Where is *home* for you? Where do you go to feel rested, completely accepted, at peace? Perhaps it's not a place but a person. When you are with this someone — maybe a best friend

173

or a parent—you just feel like you *fit*. You have nothing to prove, no unhappiness clouds your vision, and you can completely relax and let your guard down. Or maybe it's an activity, such as fly-fishing, golf, singing a particular hymn, or star-gazing. What moves you to laughter . . . or to tears?

These experiences, people, and memories are wonderful, albeit temporary, blessings from the hand of the Lord as we journey to our ultimate Home. These things can't ultimately satisfy us, of course, but they can point us to their ultimate satisfaction. C. S. Lewis calls the feeling we get when we consider these things, the sense that wells up in our inner being, an inconsolable longing. "There have been times when I think we do not desire heaven," C. S. Lewis said, "but more often I find myself wondering whether, in our heart of hearts, we have ever desired anything else. . . . It is the secret signature of each soul, the incommunicable and unappeasable want."[1]

Well, as we saw in the previous chapter, the Bible tells us that a heavenly wedding feast awaits those of us who love Jesus. At this feast we will finally be at home, gathered around the table, rejoicing in our Savior and in one another. I like to think that at the great supper the Lord will put Mama Stella to work. I can just see her making those biscuits. Yes, as Revelation 19:9 says, "Blessed are those who are invited to the marriage supper of the Lamb."

Can you imagine sitting around with loved ones, your own Mama Stellas? Can you picture passing the potatoes to outstanding believers from history, such as D. L. Moody or C. H. Spurgeon? And what about the great men and women of the Bible, such as Moses, Mary Magdalene, Stephen, or even Eutychus? Remember, these are the folks who may have been cheering you on all along. You will be able to thank them, trade stories of God's faithfulness, and talk about the endless future ahead.

But there will be someone else there. He paid for the meal, served His disciples, and has invited you to the wedding feast. In fact, He used eating as a metaphor of how He longs to have a relationship with us. "Behold," Jesus says, "I stand at the door and knock. If anyone hears my voice and opens the door, I will come in to him and eat with him, and he with me" (Rev. 3:20). Yes, we will actually have the privilege of eating with and being served by the Host Himself.

And as we sit at the table with Jesus in unhurried conversation, all of those nagging, unanswered questions will finally be dealt with. The seemingly "unfair" things in our lives will be resolved. Pain will be replaced by comfort. Tears will be replaced by joy and laughter. In Heaven, all your losses will be more than compensated for.

> Our present troubles are small and won't last very long. Yet they produce for us a glory that vastly outweighs them and will last forever! So we don't look at the troubles we can see now; rather, we fix our gaze on things that cannot be seen. For the things we see now will soon be gone, but the things we cannot see will last forever. (2 Cor. 4:17-18, NLT)

The contrast between our "present troubles" and the future "glory" is more vast than we can imagine. Randy Alcorn says that "one paragraph into chapter 1 . . . will make up for eighty hard 'chapters' on Earth, but even if it took another eighty to compensate, the joys would have only just begun."[2] The contrast is not just in the quantity of time, but also in its quality. It is the difference between light and darkness.

J. R. R. Tolkien wrote, "Frodo heard a sweet singing running in his mind: a song that seemed to come like a pale light behind a grey rain-curtain, and growing stronger to turn the veil all to glass and silver, until at last it was rolled back, and a far green country opened before him under a swift sunrise."[3] We are looking forward to an eternal sunrise.

This contrast between Heaven and earth should quicken our pulse and lighten our step. Heaven is not "pie in the sky." It is a feast we can begin to taste right now if our spiritual palate has been prepared. E. M. Bounds wrote,

> Heaven ought to draw and engage us. Heaven ought to so fill our hearts and hands, our conversations, our character, and our features, that all would see that we are foreigners, strangers to this world.

The very atmosphere of this world should be chilling to us and noxious, its suns eclipsed and its companionship dull and insipid.

Heaven is our native land and home to us, and death to us is not the dying hour, but the birth hour![4]

We have spent a book previewing Heaven and the difference it should make in our lives on earth, but there is still more to say. The first is that Heaven indeed is "for real." It's not a metaphor, a state of mind, or simply a kind of wishful thinking. Heaven exists. As Moody once said, "Heaven is just as much a place as Chicago."[5]

What *kind* of place? It is the dwelling place of God Himself, where God lives directly, unmediated, with His people for all eternity (see Rev. 21:3). God, of course, lived among us in the garden until sin sundered that relationship. God again dwelt with His people in the tabernacle and temple in ancient Israel. And Jesus, John 1:14 says, "made his home among us" during His earthly ministry (NLT). Right before He returned to the Father, Jesus promised us an eternal home: "I go and prepare a place for you" (Jn. 14:3). Heaven is the place where God dwells with us.

"Heaven is a place," wrote Bounds. "Out of the region of all fancy it is taken and put into the realm of the actual, the local. . . . . Heaven does not float around. It is not made of air, thin air. It is real, a country, a clime, a home sacred affinities draw to the spot."[6]

Scripture uses different words to describe this place we call Heaven.

Heaven is described as a *paradise*. Paul the apostle saw Heaven. Interestingly, he did *not* write a book about it! Perhaps that is because he was at a loss for words. In 2 Corinthians 12, he writes,

I know a man in Christ who fourteen years ago was caught up to the third heaven. Whether it was in the body or out of the body I do not know—God knows. And I know that this man—whether in the body or apart from the body I do not know, but God knows—was caught up to paradise and heard inexpressible things, things that no one is permitted to tell. (vv. 2-4, NIV)

Paul was saying, "Look, it is really hard for me to put into words what I saw." He used one word to describe it: *paradise*, which is very hard to translate. This is the same word that Jesus used when He told the thief on the cross, "Truly, I say to you, today you will be with me in Paradise" (Lk. 23:43).

It can be used to describe the walled garden of a king. Think of the Hanging Gardens of Babylon, the Biltmore Estate in North Carolina, or Cantigny in Illinois. These gardens had or have huge tracts of incredibly diverse, well-tended plant life. But they are not simply wild, untamed areas. Already beautiful, they are a palette for intelligent artistry. They blend the human and the natural to the glory of God. People are to bring out the beauty of these places through their work and ingenuity, as our first parents did in the Garden of Eden, to "work it and keep it" (Gen. 2:15). N. T. Wright speaks of the "human project of bringing wise order to the garden."[7] Such work on earth reflects our Creator in Heaven. God, of course, is the ultimate Gardener, but I expect we will have unlimited opportunities to cultivate the heavenly paradise, too, if we are so inclined.

At the very least, we will certainly marvel at it.

Heaven is a paradise, a place that far surpasses anything we know on earth. Paul said to his beloved Philippians, "I am torn between the two: I desire to depart and be with Christ, which is better by far" (Phil. 1:23, NIV). Paul's wording is in the superlative form. It means far, far better, or even way better.

The current popular books about people who have "died and gone to Heaven," whatever differences they exhibit when describing eternity, almost uniformly report that visitors never want to go back to earth, or return only reluctantly. In that emphasis, at least, they are absolutely right. Nobody in Heaven, if given the choice, would ever want to come back to earth again.

Think about how Paul must have felt when he was sent back. The believers have been standing around his beaten and bloodied body. Most thought they would never see him alive again. Suddenly, however, the flush of color returns to the apostle's cheeks. His eyes begin to blink. If it were me, the first thing I would have done is demand to know who prayed for me to be brought back! But Paul gets up and returns to work (see Acts 14:19-20). He leaves Paradise and does the work that God has called him to do.

Heaven is also described as a city. Hebrews 11:10 (NIV) says it is a city "with foundations, whose architect and builder is God." Hebrews 13:14 (NIV) says, "For here we do not have an enduring city, but we are looking for the city that is to come."

The Bible doesn't say that Heaven is *like* a city. It says it *is* a city. According to these two verses, Heaven has foundations, has been designed and built by God, is enduring, and will be coming. So it is a real city, but we do not see it yet. Perhaps you've read about Rome, Paris, or New York. You've read about it or heard eyewitness reports from those who have visited, but you haven't seen it with your own eyes. Still, you believe because you have good evidence. It is the same with Heaven.

According to one definition, a city is a "center of population, commerce, and culture; a town of significant size and importance."[8] Certainly the heavenly city will have a very significant population, with the redeemed from all ages. We also know there will be "people for God from every tribe and language and people and nation" (Rev. 5:9). That is a throng!

Think of the cultural possibilities of Heaven with that kind of diversity. There are thousands of languages and cultures in the world today. Now think about all the things you can do, all the places you can go, all the experiences you can have in cities: music, stores, restaurants, museums, parks, homes, theaters, and so on. The Bible says Heaven is a city, one without crime, urban decay, or crowding. It will be exciting, to say the least!

Heaven is also a *country*, the Bible says. As we have seen, Hamlet called what comes after death the "undiscovered country," with not a little foreboding. Christians, however, need not fear it and instead ought to anticipate this country joyfully. That's why Hebrews 11:16 (NIV) says that the saints of old were "longing for a better country — a heavenly one." Yes, if we have our spiritual priorities straight, we will be *longing* for Heaven . . . inconsolably. As Paul said, we are citizens not of earth, but of Heaven (see Phil. 3:20).

And the fact is, Heaven is a precursor to something even greater. Heaven, or, as we have seen, the third Heaven, isn't our final destination. A lot of well-meaning people say, "I am going to die and live forever in Heaven." Well, have fun. I for one am not staying there — I am coming back to earth with Jesus! Yes, we *will* go to Heaven when we die. But the Bible teaches that one day Christ will come back to earth and establish His kingdom and reign for a thousand years. But then there is even more for us to anticipate.

> I saw a new heaven and a new earth, for the first heaven and the first earth had passed away, and the sea was no more. And I saw the Holy City, new Jerusalem, coming down out of heaven from God, prepared as a bride adorned for her husband. And I heard a loud voice from the throne saying, "Behold, the dwelling place of God is with man. He will dwell with them, and they will be his people, and God himself will be with them as their God. He will wipe away every tear from their eyes, and death shall be no more, neither shall there be mourning, nor crying, nor pain anymore, for the former things have passed away." (Rev. 21:1-4)

This is a whole new order of existence. We will not be floating around the universe as disembodied spirits. Friend, we who believe in Christ and who have risen to meet Him in the air will have new, glorified, resurrected bodies, just as He has.

That's one reason why films such as *Ghost* are so terribly off the mark. Our eternal existence isn't going to be spectral. It will be *bodily*. Jesus has a resurrection *body*, and so will we. God's Word, you see, says Christ's resurrection on the third day is the firstfruits of our own. In ancient times, the Israelites would make a symbolic offering to the Lord of the first part of the harvest, knowing that the rest of the crop would be ready in due time. Christ's resurrection two thousand years ago is in a sense an offering to the Lord and a guarantor of the resurrection of His people.

> Christ has indeed been raised from the dead, the firstfruits of those who have fallen asleep. For since death came through a man, the resurrection of the dead comes also through a man. For as in Adam all die, so in Christ all will be made alive. But each in turn: Christ, the firstfruits; then, when he comes, those who belong to him. Then the end will come, when he hands over the kingdom to God the Father after he has destroyed all dominion, authority and power. For he must reign until he has put all his enemies under his feet. The last enemy to be destroyed is death. (1 Cor. 15:20-26, NIV)

The idea of living a resurrected existence in Heaven (or the new Heaven) has important implications for our lives on earth — "on earth as it is in Heaven." At a minimum, it means that what we do down here still matters, as it points to a perfect and fulfilled existence above. We await a heavenly land and kingdom, yes, but without disparaging the earth on which God has placed us now.

Another wonderful thing about Heaven is the fact that each of us will receive a glorified body at the resurrection. The prototype for this new body, if you will, is Jesus Christ's. He rose in a real body. In a real world. In a real way.

Think of this for a moment. Jesus has been crucified. He has told the disciples to wait for Him. Peter, however, hangs a sign on his office door: "Gone fishing." Some of the others go with him.

> They went out and got into the boat, but that night they caught nothing.
>
> Early in the morning, Jesus stood on the shore, but the disciples did not realize that it was Jesus.
>
> He called out to them, "Friends, haven't you any fish?"
>
> "No," they answered.
>
> He said, "Throw your net on the right side of the boat and you

will find some." When they did, they were unable to haul the net in because of the large number of fish.

Then the disciple whom Jesus loved said to Peter, "It is the Lord!" As soon as Simon Peter heard him say, "It is the Lord," he wrapped his outer garment around him (for he had taken it off) and jumped into the water. The other disciples followed in the boat, towing the net full of fish, for they were not far from shore, about a hundred yards. When they landed, they saw a fire of burning coals there with fish on it, and some bread.

Jesus said to them, "Bring some of the fish you have just caught." So Simon Peter climbed back into the boat and dragged the net ashore. It was full of large fish, 153, but even with so many the net was not torn. Jesus said to them, "Come and have breakfast." None of the disciples dared ask him, "Who are you?" They knew it was the Lord. Jesus came, took the bread and gave it to them, and did the same with the fish. (Jn. 21:3-13, NIV)

This seems like an ordinary scene, until we remember that Jesus has just been raised from the dead. We see a number of things about His resurrection body:

1. *Jesus was physical.* He stood on the shore. He wasn't a phantom floating around. He spoke to them with a human voice: *Do you have any fish?* He was a real person.
2. *Jesus was recognizable.* He even bore the scars of the Crucifixion, wounds that could be touched (see Jn. 20:27).
3. *Jesus did not have normal limitations.* He was able to appear and disappear at will (see Jn. 20:19). He even ascended into Heaven (see Acts 1:9). (The word used is *harpazo.*)
4. *Jesus ate food.* When He appeared to the disciples, Jesus ate a piece of broiled fish to prove to them He wasn't a ghost (see Lk. 24:41-42).

All these qualities of His body will be ours, as well. Remember, Jesus' resurrection is the firstfruits of ours. You will be physical. You will be recognizable. You will be you. But you won't have the normal limitations that your body has now. We are told, "The body that is sown is perishable, it is raised imperishable; it is sown in dishonor, it is raised in glory; it is sown in weakness, it is raised in power; it is sown a natural body, it is raised a spiritual body" (1 Cor. 15:42-44, NIV).

Yes, my friend, Heaven is a place—but is it your place? You can know for sure. When winter starts to come on, the remarkable Golden Plover leaves its breeding grounds in the Aleutian Islands and flies more than two thousand miles to Hawaii. This bird, at the start of its journey, weighs only about seven ounces. Its tiny, precise wings flap continuously over the eighty-eight-hour flight, with no stopovers. The bird has no GPS. Instead, it has an unerring homing instinct and seems divinely built for the incredible journey.[9]

The same is true for us. God has given us a homing instinct for a place *we* have never been. We have been created and built for Heaven, which is the answer to all our questions and longings. The little Plover has never been to Hawaii, yet somehow it arrives. Do you know how to get to Heaven?

Before Jesus was going to return to Heaven, the disciples were scared, and understandably so. They were in the midst of a hostile world, uncertain of the future. In that, they were much like the rest of us. They didn't want Jesus to leave.

"Lord," Thomas (later called "Doubting") said, "we do not know where you are going. How can we know the way?" The answer from Jesus: "I am the way, and the truth, and the life. No one comes to the Father except through me."[10]

Jesus, the one who came down *from* Heaven, is also the way *to* Heaven . . . but only for those who have made Him their Lord.

Have *you*?

CONVERSATION GUIDE

There may be no more fascinating subject than Heaven! This guide is designed to help you work through *As It Is in Heaven* with others in some really fantastic and soul-searching conversations. You don't have to go through every question. Just dive in and see how far you get. Also, as you'll recall, this book centers on how Heaven brings focus to what really matters in your life. After the conversation has come to a close, there are some practical suggestions for what you can do with what you have learned.

CHAPTER 1
Much Ado About Heaven

Conversation Starters

1. During *Inside the Actor's Workshop*, interviewer James Lipton asks his guests, "If Heaven exists, what would you like to hear God say when you arrive at the pearly gates?" How would you answer this question? Now, as opposed to what you hope He would say, what do you think He would say?

2. Do you believe you are going to Heaven or Hell? Or do you believe that there is nothing after death? How does your belief in what happens after you die affect how you live today?

3. How much stock should we put in media versions of Heaven? Why do you think Heaven is such a hot topic in the entertainment industry?

4. Have you ever had a near death experience? What happened? Do you think what you experienced actually happened, or do you think it came from inside yourself? How did the NDE affect your life?

5. What nagging questions do you have about Heaven? What do you think drives your curiosity about the life to come?

6. The Lord's Prayer encourages us to pray for God's will to be done on earth as it is in Heaven. Have you ever considered how life in Heaven should affect your life on earth? How is God's will done in Heaven, and how can we begin to see it done on earth?

Put It to Memory

Memorizing a few verses from the Bible is a great way to allow Scripture to encourage you throughout the day, no matter what's going on in your life.

> Our Father in heaven,
> hallowed be your name.
> Your kingdom come,
> your will be done,
>   on earth as it is in heaven.
> Give us this day our daily bread,
> and forgive us our debts,
>   as we also have forgiven our debtors.
> And lead us not into temptation,
>   but deliver us from evil. (Mt. 6:9-13)

Do Something!

The Bible tells us that we should want to do God's will. We will do this for all eternity in Heaven, so we ought to get started on earth. Think of one thing that you know is the Lord's will for you to do today, tell your pastor or a Christian friend about it, and then go do it.

CHAPTER 2
Life Is the Warm-Up Act

Conversation Starters

1. What are your life plans, and do they take into account the reality of eternity? How might you change them so they reflect the fact that our earthly existence is merely a blip when compared with the everlasting nature of Heaven and Hell?

2. Greg Laurie says, "What we do down here matters, and in fact it sets our course for our eternity—for good or for ill." Reflect quietly on this quote for a minute or two. What comes to mind?

3. One poll says that many Americans believe that our life goals ought to be enjoyment and personal fulfillment. What do you think are better goals and why?

4. Greg says that God is worthy of our worship because He created us. How does that make you feel? How might your relationship with the Lord reflect that He's your creator?

5. People in our society often act as though the meaning of life is unknowable, but that's not what the Bible says. According to Revelation 4:11, what is the meaning of life? What does this truth say to those who seek their *own* glory and pleasure? How can we tell what is most important to a person? Why is putting God first far better than putting *self* first?

6. According to Greg, why is the pursuit of pleasure a "monster"? What examples of this truth does he share? Can you think of any of your own?

7. Greg says, "The key to a full and joyful life on earth is a heavenly focus on the glory of God." Have you experienced this truth in your own life? Why do you think it's true? How might you begin to focus on God and His glory?

8. Heaven will be full of joyful worship of the triune God. Does that prospect thrill you or frighten you? Is worship easy or hard for you? (Be honest.)

Put It to Memory

Memorizing a few verses from the Bible is a great way to allow Scripture to encourage you throughout the day, no matter what's going on in your life.

> Worthy are you, our Lord and God,
>> to receive glory and honor and power,
> for you created all things,
>> and by your will they existed and were created. (Rev. 4:11)

Do Something!

It's hard to worship God when we cannot see Him. Yet Jesus Christ is "the image of the invisible God" (Col. 1:15). Read John 4 and list the truths about God you see displayed in Christ's ministry. Then spend a few minutes prayerfully thanking God for each one.

CHAPTER 3
The Man from Heaven

Conversation Starters

1. Who's the world's preeminent authority on fashion? Physics? Mathematics? Retirement planning? Gardening? Mexican cooking? Would you trust someone in any of these areas who does not possess firsthand experience? Why or why not? What relevance might this insight have for the subject of Heaven?

2. Is "new" always "improved"? Why or why not? Can you think of any examples when a new item or model was inferior to the old? Why do we so often indulge ourselves in what C. S. Lewis called "chronological snobbery"? What is the danger?

3. Many religious figures have said there is life beyond the grave. Can you summarize what some of them have said? What about the teaching of Jesus? How is Christ's teaching uniquely authoritative? Why do we have good reason to believe He was telling the truth?

4. What does Greg say "is an example of Heaven turning the old earthly order of sin and death upside down and inside out, ending the dreary reign of the second law of thermodynamics"? What are some of the evidences we have for Christ's physical, space-time resurrection from the dead, and what do they tell us about Heaven?

5. What does Jesus teach about marriage in Heaven? Why might human marriage be a temporary institution? Does His teaching make our earthly relationships more important or less? Explain your answer.

6. Greg says that we need to get past the question, "Am I going to live forever?" to focus on this one: "*Where* am I going to live forever?" Why is it so difficult for us to make this adjustment?

Put It to Memory

Memorizing a few verses from the Bible is a great way to allow Scripture to encourage you throughout the day, no matter what's going on in your life.

> Enter by the narrow gate. For the gate is wide and the way is easy that leads to destruction, and those who enter by it are many. For

the gate is narrow and the way is hard that leads to life, and those who find it are few. (Mt. 7:13-14)

Do Something!

Write out in a hundred words or fewer how Christ has changed your life. If He hasn't changed it yet, write about how you wish He could. Share it with a Christian friend and ask for his or her honest critique. If you don't have a Christian friend, pray for God to give you one.

CHAPTER 4
A Hopeful Heaven

Conversation Starters

1. Have you experienced the death of someone close to you? How did you feel when this happened? How have your feelings changed as time has passed? What has surprised you or stood out in the process of grieving for this loved one? Do you believe that the experience has helped you prepare for the next time? What "unfinished business" do you have?

2. Have you ever been told that God will protect His children from all harm? How has this statement stacked up to your personal reality? How did you respond? How has Greg's sharing on the struggles he faced with his family members shaped your own thinking?

3. Greg says that God's children will experience an "expected end," even though day by day we can't always tell what He is doing. "God, the premier Artist, is working on a canvas," Greg writes. "That canvas is you. Day by day he adds to it, with a line here, a bit of shading there, a splash of color another time." How have you seen the premier Artist working on your life canvas, and have you yet discovered why He was doing it?

4. When Greg gets depressed about his son Christopher, he preaches to himself, remembering God's promises and character. He says people might look at him and think he is crazy but that he is a "hopeful lunatic!" How does trust in the Lord sometimes look strange in this world? Are you ready to look strange in order to trust in Him?

5. When something bad happens to us, why are we *not* to ask why? How do we learn from the appeal of Mary and Martha about how we ought to approach the Lord in times of trouble? How is this approach different from what we might expect?

6. Have you ever had to wait for God's answer to your prayer? How did the delay either weaken or strengthen your faith? Did it make you run *toward* Jesus or *away* from Him?

7. "If something breaks *your* heart," Greg says, "it breaks *His* as well." Many people say that God is an unfeeling, demanding "eye in the sky" who keeps track of our sins but is never around when we need Him. How do Jesus' tears discount this perspective?

8. How does Greg say we should respond when our prayers go unanswered? What grounds does he give us to hope even in the midst of painful trials, such as the loss of loved ones? If Jesus really *is* the resurrection and the life, how ought this truth change our lives today?

Put It to Memory

Memorizing a few verses from the Bible is a great way to allow Scripture to encourage you throughout the day, no matter what's going on in your life.

> Jesus said to her, "I am the resurrection and the life. Whoever believes in me, though he die, yet shall he live, and everyone who lives and believes in me shall never die. Do you believe this?" (Jn. 11:25-26)

Do Something!

Visit a friend in a nursing home, hospital, or hospice and read John 11 aloud together. Then share what you've learned from this chapter about how Jesus can deliver us from the fear of death.

CHAPTER 5
Flying over Heaven

Conversation Starters

1. Popular conceptions of Heaven abound, but they always come up short of reality. Why? According to Greg, what is our surest guide to what Heaven is like? Are you more inclined to read a contemporary eyewitness account or the Bible? Explain your answer.

2. The Bible says there are *three* Heavens. What are they? What roles do they perform? Why can none of us see the third Heaven? Are you less inclined to believe in it because you cannot see it?

3. What are some of the pictures that prophets such as Ezekiel and Isaiah employ to describe heavenly realities? How are these approximations like Heaven?

4. What kind of rewards have you grown accustomed to in this earthly life? Does it surprise you that there will be heavenly rewards too? Does that create in you a sense of anticipation or dread? What will we do with our crowns?

5. How, according to Greg, will Heaven give us a sense of perspective about our earthly lives? How was this true for Job? For John the apostle? For you? What questions would you like to have answered by God?

6. When you think of the word *worship*, what first comes to mind? Are you excited, bored, or something in between? Why, according to Greg, *won't* worship in Heaven be boring? What are some earthly examples that point to this truth? How might you change your attitude about worship so that it's about what you *give* rather than what you *get*?

7. What do you like about work? Dislike? Greg points out that we will work in Heaven. Does that disappoint you or excite you? How might our heavenly service differ from our earthly tasks? What kinds of work would you be interested in doing for God in eternity?

8. How is our giving a clear barometer of our spirituality? Does your giving reflect Heaven's priorities or your own?

9. Are you "walking with God"? Do you want to be? What's the first step for you?

Put It to Memory

Memorizing a few verses from the Bible is a great way to allow Scripture to encourage you throughout the day, no matter what's going on in your life.

> After this I looked, and behold, a great multitude that no one could number, from every nation, from all tribes and peoples and languages, standing before the throne and before the Lamb, clothed in white robes, with palm branches in their hands, and crying out with a loud voice, "Salvation belongs to our God who sits on the throne, and to the Lamb!" (Rev. 7:9-10)

Do Something!

God's glory is something that Christians talk about often, but what does it really mean? Get together with a group of friends to really talk about God's glory as it's described in this chapter. At the end of your time, see if you can come up with several practical ways in which you can give glory to God each day in the week ahead.

CHAPTER 6
What Heaven Knows About Earth

Conversation Starters

1. Do you agree with the statement "One of the keys to happiness is a bad memory"? Why or why not? What role do memories play in our experiencing full and happy lives? Do you believe that God will wipe away our memories in Heaven (at least the bad ones)? What does Greg say about this? What memories would you like to have wiped clean?

2. Puritan Richard Baxter wrote of a "delightful complacency" of the saved in Heaven. How has this idea been twisted in American history into a fear that we will have spiritual amnesia in the afterlife—that we will somehow be less than we are now? What evidence does Greg offer to refute this view?

3. "Our fear of boredom in Heaven reflects a lack of holy imagination on our part," Greg writes, "not a lack of excitement on Heaven's part. We will be fully engaged in heavenly worship, and, even more thrilling, we will have an eye on earth as well. That perception will help us appreciate God's grace in eternally meaningful ways." Describe a time when you were fully engaged in activity you really loved. Does this help you anticipate Heaven in a new way?

4. "We won't know *less* in Heaven than we know on earth," Greg asserts. "We'll know *more*." What are some of the things we'll know if we belong to Christ? What will be the same about us? What are some of the things we'll pray for? Do we pray for those things *now*?

5. What would you like to remember in Heaven? What would you like to forget?

6. The Bible also says that people will be fully conscious in Hell — no soul sleep or annihilation. What does Luke 16 teach about this awful but true future for all who do not belong to Jesus Christ? How do we know whether we are headed for Heaven or Hell? Do we get a second chance after death?

7. Does God want you to go to Heaven or Hell? How do you know? Share a verse that tells us this. Have you decided to trust in Jesus so that you can go to Heaven when you die? Do you know for sure where you will live in eternity? What about your loved ones? What are you waiting for in sharing the good news?

8. Are you afraid of death? Why not receive Christ's offer of salvation through His death and resurrection by placing your faith in Him today?

Put It to Memory

Memorizing a few verses from the Bible is a great way to allow Scripture to encourage you throughout the day, no matter what's going on in your life.

> Working together with him, then, we appeal to you not to receive the grace of God in vain. For he says,
>
> "In a favorable time I listened to you,
>   and in a day of salvation I have helped you."
>
> Behold, now is the favorable time; behold, now is the day of salvation. (2 Cor. 6:1-2)

Do Something!

Take a piece of paper and write down your three happiest memories in a short paragraph. They could be from when you were a child, got married, found a job, or went to a concert. They could be silly or profound, serious or strange. All that matters is that they made you happy. Now spend a few minutes thanking God for each one and for the fact that He cares about such things.

CHAPTER 7
When Seeing Is Believing

Conversation Starters

1. John the apostle was a spiritually perceptive person who had an especially close relationship with Jesus. Who are some of your closest friends? What makes you click as friends? Have you been able to encourage one another in your search for spiritual truth?

2. In discussing the necessity of faith, Greg asks, "Why was Jesus' identity so often hidden behind His humility? Why didn't He just make it plain? Why not simply burst into the world with miraculous power and finish the job?" What do *you* think?

3. What is it like to always have to believe even when we cannot see (see Heb. 11:1)? Truth be told, does exercising faith ever get tiring? Can you picture your relief when "seeing is believing"? What do you most want to see when you get to Heaven?

4. Many today have an opinion about Jesus—that He was a prophet, a revolutionary, a good teacher who got in over His head, or even the Son of God. What's your opinion? Why is it important to hear from Jesus Himself about His identity? What insights can we gain from His own words?

5. Have you ever been hurt or let down by a false witness? What does it mean that Jesus is the "faithful witness"? How is speaking the truth in love different from being brutally honest?

6. How does God's everlasting love give us confidence before Him? How did He tangibly demonstrate His love for us? What did you do to deserve this love? How does that affect your understanding of God and yourself?

7. Greg says, "Jesus, who came incognito the first time, will come in unmistakable power and great glory the final time." In other words, for those who believe, seeing *will* be believing, faith will be sight, and hope will be consummation. Are you ready to exercise your faith now, *before* Jesus comes in power and great glory? Are you willing to wait in quiet faith?

Put It to Memory

Memorizing a few verses from the Bible is a great way to allow Scripture to encourage you throughout the day, no matter what's going on in your life.

> Then I turned to see the voice that was speaking to me, and on turning I saw seven golden lampstands, and in the midst of the lampstands one like a son of man, clothed with a long robe and with a golden sash around his chest. The hairs of his head were white, like white wool, like snow. His eyes were like a flame of fire, his feet were like burnished bronze, refined in a furnace, and his voice was like the roar of many waters. In his right hand he held seven stars, from his mouth came a sharp two-edged sword, and his face was like the sun shining in full strength. (Rev. 1:12-16)

Do Something!

Take a piece of paper and jot down any situations from the last week in which you have lied, in ways big or small, to protect yourself. Ask God to forgive you. Where possible, seek to make amends with anyone you have hurt.

CHAPTER 8
Heaven's Messengers

Conversation Starters

1. Do you believe in the existence of angels and demons? On what basis? Why do you think so many people, in our supposedly scientific and enlightened age, do? Have you ever seen angels at work?

2. The universe that God has made — in Heaven and on earth — has different kinds of created beings: people made in God's image, animals, and angels. Why might God allow for such diversity in His created order? Is there any reason angels should not or could not be created in God's world?

3. When was the most frightened you have ever felt? The poet Rainer Maria Rilke said, "Every angel is terrifying." Do you feel that way? Why or why not? Do you think the natural fear human beings experience in the presence of angels reflects our lesser power, our greater sin, or both?

4. What does the presence of angels have to do with our prayers? How does this truth inform our faith when God's answers seem delayed? Why do you think God sometimes uses angels when working out His will? Why do you think He sometimes uses *us*?

5. Greg writes, "The angels and those who have gone on to Heaven before us have the unspeakable privilege of experiencing the face of God right now. Whatever else Heaven offers — and all this is beyond human comprehension — it holds out the incredible promise that we too will one day see the face of God." Take a moment or two to consider what seeing that face might be like. Share with the group as you feel comfortable.

6. Angels, Greg notes, are not celestial robots. They have emotions and worship God, too. What does this truth do for your own sense of worship? Does it make you want to worship the Lord *more*?

7. Why does God not simply do the more efficient thing and get angels — rather than people — to run all His errands? What does this tell us about His love for His people?

Put It to Memory

Memorizing a few verses from the Bible is a great way to allow Scripture to encourage you throughout the day, no matter what's going on in your life.

> Are they not all ministering spirits sent out to serve for the sake of those who are to inherit salvation? (Heb. 1:14)

Do Something!

Choose a cultural depiction of angels (music, film, TV, book) and share it with the group. Discuss what it gets wrong and right about angels.

CHAPTER 9
Heaven's Heroes

Conversation Starters

1. Greg asks, "Have you ever been persecuted for your faith in Christ, or do you know someone who has? I don't mean laughed at, ridiculed, or ignored. . . . What I'm talking about is the possible loss of a friendship, your marriage, a job, your health, your money, or even your life—not because you were rude or thoughtless in how you shared the gospel but because you were a Christian." Tell about a time when this happened to you.

2. How much do you know about persecuted Christians in other parts of the world? Share with the group an experience you had of praying for them, giving money for their relief, or speaking up on their behalf to your elected representatives. Do you find it hard to consistently care about these brothers and sisters?

3. Why is the persecution of believers on earth front-page news in Heaven? How can this knowledge spur us on to greater passion and compassion concerning persecution as we focus on this issue in our homes, small groups, churches, and Christian ministries?

4. Why is the cry for justice a Heavenly virtue? How does justice express God's will being done on earth as it is in Heaven? How actively do matters of justice concern your soul? What are some issues of justice that you feel called and equipped to address in your own life?

5. Why, according to Greg (and the apostle Paul), did God give us the law? How do we, as God's Heaven-bound people, avoid using the law as a way to confirm us in our self-righteousness? How does the law deepen our sense of personal sin?

6. How are God's holiness and His mercy both expressions of His character? Which one resonates more with you? How does each aspect balance out the other? How did God bring them together in Jesus Christ? How often do you think about Hell?

7. How does suffering sometimes force us to put one foot in Heaven and one on earth? Why is a longing for Heaven in the midst of painful circumstances not mere escapism? How has the truth of Heaven helped you or someone you know get through hard times?

8. In Heaven, we will be reunited with those we helped bring to faith. How is this an encouragement to do evangelism and also to trust God?

Put It to Memory

Memorizing a few verses from the Bible is a great way to allow Scripture to encourage you throughout the day, no matter what's going on in your life.

> All who desire to live a godly life in Christ Jesus will be persecuted. (2 Tim. 3:12)

Do Something!

From a magazine such as *Christianity Today* or *World*, take a current article about Christians anywhere in the world being persecuted. Share the highlights with your group. Then pray about what you have read, asking for God to give justice to His saints and salvation to the persecutors.

CHAPTER 10
A Royal Cheering Section

Conversation Starters

1. Do you believe that you'll be reunited with departed loved ones when you die? On what basis do you believe this? Do you agree with Billy Graham that we and they need to be Christians in order for this reunion to take place? What will be the first thing you say to your loved ones?

2. In Hebrews 12, we are treated to a scene in a heavenly stadium. We are not among the spectators. Instead, we are the competing athletes. Those in the stadium are watching *us* and *our* progress in the gospel. If you're a runner or any other type of performer, do you try just a little bit harder when someone's eye is on you? How about when those in Heaven are watching?

3. Greg talks about us *finishing* the race, not *winning* it. How does this distinction help you understand the lifelong task of discipleship? How is the Christian life more like a marathon and less like a sprint? Why is finishing more important than winning?

4. Who are some of the saints cheering us on in the race of faith (see Hebrews 11)? Which ones are your favorites, and why? What people do you think might be with them in the stands? How might they be cheering *you* on today? How does that encourage you to keep going?

5. If someone were to objectively evaluate your life, do you think you would be seen as a people-pleaser or a God-pleaser? Why? Cite an example. What is your focus: Heaven or earth?

6. By faith, Noah looked foolish for the Lord for a very long time. Why do you think he was able to stick with it for so long? How is his example an encouragement to you to keep going? What might the Lord be asking you to do that, in the world's eyes, looks a bit foolish?

7. Abraham is perhaps the prototypical example in the Bible of faith (see Gen. 12:1-3). Yet in Hebrews 11, he is commended for his faithful *obedience*. What is the connection between faith and works? Cite a Bible verse to support your position. How might you exhibit faith the way Abraham, the heavenly witness, did?

8. How is Jesus the ultimate heavenly witness? How does His example inspire you to run the race with endurance? Why is the finish line to which He calls us our *real* home?

Put It to Memory

Memorizing a few verses from the Bible is a great way to allow Scripture to encourage you throughout the day, no matter what's going on in your life.

> Since we are surrounded by so great a cloud of witnesses, let us also lay aside every weight, and sin which clings so closely, and let us run with endurance the race that is set before us, looking to Jesus, the founder and perfecter of our faith, who for the joy that was set before him endured the cross, despising the shame, and is seated at the right hand of the throne of God. (Heb. 12:1-2)

Do Something!

In a time of reflective prayer, consider departed loved ones who know the Lord. Take time to thank God that these and other saints are cheering you on right now.

CHAPTER 11
Party Time

Conversation Starters

1. The similarities between Billy Graham and an unknown Sunday school teacher named Edward Kimball are amazing. If you're a believer, what one person was most instrumental in your salvation? In his or hers? How far back can you go in your personal chain of salvation? Do you ever wonder who will be a Christian in future generations thanks to your faithful witness today?

2. What do you really enjoy about telling others the good news? What frightens you? Is there anything keeping you from being a more consistent witness for Jesus Christ? What steps could you take this week to address this challenge?

3. Jesus embraced sinners, giving them His time and attention, which scandalized the Pharisees. It's easy to condemn the Pharisees for their hard-heartedness, but do our weekly schedules more reflect Jesus' concern for the outcasts or the Pharisees' neglect? What can we do to more closely align our priorities with those of Jesus?

4. Jesus tells three stories: about a lost sheep, a lost coin, and a lost son. What is similar about them? What is different? Which story touches you the most, and why?

5. Do you like to go to parties? Would you rather organize one or be a guest? Why is throwing a party a particularly appropriate response when you've found something you've lost?

6. Do you really think Heaven throws a party whenever someone comes to faith? Give three reasons this is so. Have you ever thrown a party for a new believer? What might be analogous to a party in the church when someone comes to faith?

7. For whom are you waiting to come to faith in Christ? If and when they do, will you be willing to express your happiness with a party? What would it be like, and who would be on the invitation list?

8. How does this chapter remind you of the incomparable worth of a single person (in God's eyes and also in our own)? How does it discourage us from the tyranny of numbers?

Put It to Memory

Memorizing a few verses from the Bible is a great way to allow Scripture to encourage you throughout the day, no matter what's going on in your life.

> There will be more joy in heaven over one sinner who repents than over ninety-nine righteous persons who need no repentance. (Lk. 15:7)

Do Something!

If someone in your group or church has become a Christian recently, throw him or her a party to celebrate. Be sure to invite anyone you know who would be interested. You might be surprised who shows up.

CHAPTER 12
In the Twinkling of an Eye

Conversation Starters

1. Describe a time when you were on the edge of your seat waiting for something to happen. Maybe it was a call about a job. Perhaps a baby was on the way. Maybe a doctor was going to let you know about some test results. Whatever it was, how did you feel before the event happened? After?

2. What, according to Greg, is "the next event on the prophetic calendar"? Why is it called "the blessed hope"? Do you look at it that way? Why or why not? Do you believe that Jesus could come for His own at any second? "Are you prepared for that awesome event," Greg asks, "that the Bible says will happen 'in the twinkling of an eye'?"

3. What are some arguments commonly used against belief in the Rapture as a coming event for believers? What are the answers Greg uses to address them?

4. "Some people say it doesn't really matter if you believe in the Rapture or if you think it is the same as the Second Coming," Greg says. "The fact is, it matters a lot what you believe about these things." What reasons does he give? Do they convince you? Why or why not?

5. What examples does Greg give for the concept of "rapture" from the Bible? Why might God desire to snatch his children out of trouble? According to Scripture, what happens to our bodies and spirits?

6. *When* will Christ return for His own? Can we know the day or the hour? Give reasons. *What* can we know? *How* does this knowledge help us while we wait?

7. What happens *after* the Rapture on the prophetic calendar? Are you prepared?

Put It to Memory

Memorizing a few verses from the Bible is a great way to allow Scripture to encourage you throughout the day, no matter what's going on in your life.

> Behold! I tell you a mystery. We shall not all sleep, but we shall all be changed, in a moment, in the twinkling of an eye, at the last trumpet. For the trumpet will sound, and the dead will be raised imperishable, and we shall be changed. (1 Cor. 15:51-52)

Do Something!

Borrow or buy a study Bible, and in each of the four gospels, find a time Jesus spoke of His coming again. Does the idea of Jesus' coming back excite you? Can you say with John, "Amen. Come, Lord Jesus!" (Rev. 22:20)?

CHAPTER 13
Here Comes the Judge

Conversation Starters

1. Do you sometimes think, *If only I had a better [pick one: home life, education, body], I would be a better person?* What's stopping you from being your best right now?

2. The Millennium will bring universal peace, health, longevity, harmony with nature, justice, righteousness, and holiness. "Despite all these blessings in the Millennium, amazingly, there is going to be a rebellion of mankind against God," Greg says. "Fast-forward a thousand years. There will be a final rebellion of mankind against God, then judgment." Why would people rebel against God in a perfect environment?

3. Greg describes some of the excuses people make for their sins. They say, "Well, God knows my heart," yet their heart is actually the heart of the problem! Have you ever come face-to-face with your own utter wickedness, or are you still papering over it? What is the cure for our terminal moral sickness?

4. Do you ever feel that your parents failed you or that you have failed your children? How does the rebellion at the end of the Millennium speak to this perception? How does the fact that some of God's children in the Bible also failed miserably speak to this?

5. When we stand before the Great White Throne, the time for excuses will be over. What excuses have been holding you back from turning from your sin and turning toward God? Why not be done with your excuses right now?

6. Think about what sins you will be most embarrassed about if they were brought to life. They *will* be exposed, one way or another. Why not forsake them now, while there is still time, rather than cling to them too long, allowing them to drag you under God's judgment like a millstone tied around your neck?

7. Greg says that, contrary to popular opinion, "Heaven is not the default setting for every person." Hell is the default setting, and those who don't believe in Christ will be thrown into a fearsome, everlasting lake of fire. It is the worst punishment imaginable. Yet God has done something amazing so that our default setting can be overridden. What is that, and have you received this for yourself?

8. Thinking about God's judgment ought to spur us on in evangelism. "Is there someone you are thinking of right now," Greg asks, "with whom you need to have that conversation about Jesus?" Is there? If so, pray about it and then go tell him or her the *good* news.

Put It to Memory

Memorizing a few verses from the Bible is a great way to allow Scripture to encourage you throughout the day, no matter what's going on in your life.

> Examine yourselves, to see whether you are in the faith. Test yourselves. Or do you not realize this about yourselves, that Jesus Christ is in you? — unless indeed you fail to meet the test! (2 Cor. 13:5)

Do Something!

Go to a friend or loved one who doesn't know anything about Christ, ask for permission to discuss Him and His sacrificial death on the cross for sin, and urge that person to receive Christ's gracious gift.

CHAPTER 14
Heaven's Rewards

Conversation Starters

1. What are some of the good things that have happened in the world in the delay between the Lord's first Advent and His return for His own? Why is His delay a cause for thanksgiving?

2. "Jesus' future coming should impact the way we live now," Greg says. "A desire for Heaven ought to motivate what we do on earth." Does a desire for Heaven affect your life on earth? Describe two or three examples.

3. Greg says that we will receive rewards based upon our faithful service for God. Does the prospect of rewards excite you and spur you on to ever greater levels of service? Or does it dispirit you because you're afraid you won't measure up? Why are heavenly rewards no occasion for boasting?

4. How does our attitude help us use the concept of rewards to pursue God rather than the rewards themselves? How do we change our attitude to be God-focused rather than self-focused? Why do our rewards have meaning only if they are tethered to Him?

5. Greg says that one of our rewards is our crown, which represents our ruling with the Lord. In what areas of your life are you already ruling, and how might God use that experience to prepare you for ruling with Him one day? How does your daily work fit in with this coming heavenly reality?

6. How, according to Greg, are we to wait for our Master's return? How are we to be lights, watching, expectantly waiting, and working until He comes? Do these points characterize your own life and ministry?

7. What are some of the blessings that come—in this life and the next—for those who are awaiting Christ's return? Why do we find it so hard to wait? Are you ready?

Put It to Memory

Memorizing a few verses from the Bible is a great way to allow Scripture to encourage you throughout the day, no matter what's going on in your life.

> Behold, I am coming soon, bringing my recompense with me, to repay each one for what he has done. (Rev. 22:12)

Do Something!

Describe the greatest reward you ever earned. Maybe it was a promotion or raise at work. Perhaps it was a cake your mom baked you for the good job you did on a chore. Or maybe you won a vacation for exceeding your sales goals! Now think for a minute about the everlasting rewards awaiting you for serving Jesus. Spend a minute thanking God for them and especially for allowing you access to the greatest reward: the Lord Himself.

CHAPTER 15
Christ's Resurrection — and Ours

Conversation Starters

1. Where was your favorite place during your childhood? What was so special about it? Have you traveled back there after you grew up? How had it changed? What feelings does it evoke even now? How does it point you to your heavenly home?

2. Greg asks whether you are looking forward to feasting with loved ones and great saints from the Bible. What will you want to ask them? What do you think they will want to ask *you*?

3. In *If God Is Good*, Randy Alcorn says that "one paragraph into chapter 1 . . . will make up for eighty hard 'chapters' on Earth, but even if it took another eighty to compensate, the joys would have only just begun." How does the prospect of eternal joy more than compensate for our "light momentary affliction" (2 Cor. 4:17) on this earth?

4. "This contrast between Heaven and earth should quicken our pulse and lighten our step," Greg writes. "Heaven is not 'pie in the sky.' It is a feast we can begin to taste right now if our spiritual palate has been prepared." Do you hunger for Heaven?

5. Heaven is a place that is just as real as Chicago or Sacramento. Greg says that Heaven is a cultivated paradise, a rich and diverse city, a joyful country, and a waiting area for something even better. How do these descriptions whet your appetite for Heaven?

6. Many depictions of Heaven in pop culture suggest that it will be a ghostly existence. The Bible, however, says that Christian believers can look forward to a bodily resurrection, modeled after Christ's. How does this truth about Heaven inform what we do on this earth now? How does it give hope to those who have disability or disease? How does it answer our fear of death?

Put It to Memory

Memorizing a few verses from the Bible is a great way to allow Scripture to encourage you throughout the day, no matter what's going on in your life.

I saw a new heaven and a new earth, for the first heaven and the first earth had passed away, and the sea was no more. And I saw the holy city, new Jerusalem, coming down out of heaven from God, prepared as a bride adorned for her husband. (Rev. 21:1-2)

Do Something!

Write down a list of five friends or relatives you think would be curious about Heaven. Commit to finding opportunities to share with them some of what you've learned in this book. Be ready to go deeper with them as they feel comfortable doing so.

NOTES

Chapter 1: Much Ado About Heaven

1. "Inside the Actors Studio," Wikipedia, http://en.wikipedia.org/wiki/Inside_the_Actors_Studio, accessed May 7, 2013.
2. Frank Newport, "Americans More Likely to Believe in God than the Devil, Heaven More than Hell," Gallup.com, June 13, 2007, http://www.gallup.com/poll/27877/americans-more-likely -believe-god-than-devil-Heaven-more-than-Hell.aspx, accessed May 7, 2013.
3. Gene Veith, "If you died tonight, do you know you would go to Heaven? Or do you not care?" *Cranach: The Blog of Veith*, March 15, 2012, http://www.patheos.com/blogs/geneveith/2012/03/ if-you-died-tonight-do-you-know-you-would-go-to-Heaven-or -do-you-not-care/, accessed May 7, 2013.
4. Alan Hippleheuser, "Top 10 near-death experience (NDE) books: Elisabeth Kübler Ross, *On Life After Death*," September 3, 2009, http://www.examiner.com/article/top-ten-near-death -experience-nde-books-elisabeth-k-bler-ross-on-life-after-death, accessed May 7, 2013.
5. Dinesh D'Souza, *Life After Death: The Evidence* (Washington, D.C.: Regnery, 2009), 59–60.
6. Don Piper, "What I Saw in Heaven," Beliefnet.com, http://www .beliefnet.com/Faiths/Christianity/2007/03/What-I-Saw-In -Heaven.aspx#, accessed May 7, 2013.

7. Todd Burpo, *Heaven Is for Real: A Little Boy's Astounding Story of His Trip to Heaven and Back* (Nashville: Nelson, 2010), xvii.
8. Mary C. Neal, *To Heaven and Back: A Doctor's Extraordinary Account of Her Death, Angels, and Life Again* (Colorado Springs, CO: WaterBrook, 2011), 70–71.
9. John Ortberg, *Who Is This Man? The Unpredictable Impact of the Inescapable Jesus* (Grand Rapids, MI: Zondervan, 2012), 11.

Chapter 2: Life Is the Warm-Up Act

1. Quoted in "Eternity Sermon Illustrations," http://www .moreillustrations.com/Illustrations/eternity.html, accessed May 9, 2013.
2. Greg Laurie, "Searching for Meaning," *The L.A. Christian Magazine*, http://thelachristianmagazine.com/?p=284, accessed June 17, 2013.
3. My paraphrase of the King James Version.
4. Quoted in Lesley-Ann Jones, *Mercury: An Intimate Biography of Freddie Mercury* (New York: Touchstone, 2011), 153.
5. Quoted in Lesley-Ann Jones, "Remembering Freddie Mercury," The Blog, November 23, 2011, http://www.huffingtonpost .co.uk/lesleyann-jones/freddie-mercury-remembering_b _1109533.html, accessed May 9, 2013.
6. *Westminster Shorter Catechism*, http://www.reformed.org/ documents/WSC.html, accessed May 9, 2013.

Chapter 3: The Man from Heaven

1. Quoted in http://www.celebatheists.com/wiki/Natalie_Portman, accessed May 15, 2013.
2. Quoted in GoodReads, http://www.goodreads.com/ quotes/190391-i-don-t-believe-in-happy-endings-but-i-do -believe, accessed May 15, 2013.
3. Quoted in http://www.celebatheists.com/wiki/William_Shatner, accessed May 15, 2013.
4. Quoted in The Quotations Page, http://www.quotationspage

.com/quote/24312.html, accessed May 15, 2013.

5. C. S. Lewis, *The Complete C. S. Lewis Signature Classics* (New York: HarperCollins, 2002), 36.

6. Michka Assayas, "Bono Interview: Grace Over Karma," http://www.thepoachedegg.net/the-poached-egg/2010/09/bono-interview-grace-over-karma.html, accessed July 1, 2013.

7. Dinesh D'Souza, *What's So Great about Christianity* (Carol Stream, IL: Tyndale, 2007), 301.

8. N. T. Wright, *The Resurrection of the Son of God* (Minneapolis: Fortress, 2003), 710.

9. Randy Alcorn, *Heaven* (Carol Stream, IL: Tyndale, 2004), 350.

10. Alcorn, 351.

11. Paraphrased from http://www.sermoncentral.com/sermons/communion-meditation-no-5the-fourfold-look-herman-abrahams-sermon-on-lords-supper-81357.asp?page=2, accessed May 15, 2013.

Chapter 4: A Hopeful Heaven

1. Alister E. McGrath, *A Brief History of Heaven* (Malden, MA: Blackwell, 2003), 140–141.

Chapter 5: Flying over Heaven

1. "Minister Billy Graham," http://www.ahajokes.com/reg32.html, accessed May 13, 2013.

2. Jesus Christ, of course, is the ultimate eyewitness to Heaven (see chapter 3).

3. Mary C. Neal, *To Heaven and Back: A Doctor's Extraordinary Account of Her Death, Angels, and Life Again* (Colorado Springs, CO: WaterBrook, 2011), 73.

4. Todd Burpo, *Heaven Is for Real: A Little Boy's Astounding Story of His Trip to Heaven and Back* (Nashville: Nelson, 2010), 72.

5. Alister E. McGrath, *A Brief History of Heaven* (Malden, MA: Blackwell, 2003), 3.

6. Lisa Miller, *Heaven: Our Enduring Fascination with the Afterlife*

(New York: Harper, 2010), xiv–xv.

7. C. S. Lewis, *The Complete C. S. Lewis Signature Classics* (New York: HarperCollins, 2002), 419–420.

8. International Space Hall of Fame, "Yuri A. Gagarin," New Mexico Museum of Space History, http://www.nmspacemuseum.org/halloffame/detail.php?id=8, accessed May 13, 2013.

Chapter 6: What Heaven Knows About Earth

1. "*Men in Black* (1997) Quotes," Internet Movie Database (IMDb), http://www.imdb.com/title/tt0119654/quotes, accessed May 17, 2013.

2. GoodReads, http://www.goodreads.com/quotes/tag/memory, accessed May 17, 2013.

3. Alister E. McGrath, *A Brief History of Heaven* (Malden, MA: Blackwell, 2003), 144.

4. McGrath, 150.

5. McGrath, 151.

6. Joni Eareckson Tada, *Heaven: Your Real Home* (Grand Rapids, MI: Zondervan, 1995), 19–20.

7. This is not a parable. Unlike every parable that the Lord told, this account gives names to some of its characters. They were (and are) real people.

Chapter 7: When Seeing Is Believing

1. C. S. Lewis, *The Complete C. S. Lewis Signature Classics* (New York: HarperCollins, 2002), 42.

2. Oliver Libaw, "How Widespread Is Lying in America?" ABC News, July 2 (no year provided), http://abcnews.go.com/US/story?id=92966&page=1#.UZuhDrVQHZg, accessed May 21, 2013.

3. George Orwell, "In Front of Your Nose," quoted at http://orwell.ru/library/articles/nose/english/e_nose, accessed May 21, 2013.

Chapter 8: Heaven's Messengers

1. "Dark Energy, Dark Matter," National Aeronautics and Space Administration, no date provided, http://science.nasa.gov/astrophysics/focus-areas/what-is-dark-energy/, accessed July 8, 2013.

2. Nancy Gibbs, "Angels Among Us" *Time*, December 27, 1993, http://www.time.com/time/magazine/article/0,9171,979893-9,00.html#ixzz0gavW9pJj (subscription required for online access), accessed May 22, 2013.

3. Lisa Miller, *Heaven: Our Enduring Fascination with the Afterlife* (New York: Harper, 2010), 4.

4. Billy Graham, *Angels: God's Secret Agents* (Nashville: Nelson, 2007), 5.

5. Walter A. Elwell, "Cherub, Cherubim," *Baker Encyclopedia of the Bible*, Volume 1 (Grand Rapids, MI: Baker, 1988), 428.

6. Elwell, *Encyclopedia*, Volume 1, 428.

7. John MacArthur, *The Glory of Heaven: The Truth about Heaven, Angels, and Eternal Life*, Second Edition (Wheaton, IL: Crossway, 2013), 169.

8. John F. Wade, "O Come, All Ye Faithful," ca. 1743, http://cyberhymnal.org/htm/o/c/ocomeayf.htm, accessed May 24, 2013.

9. MacArthur, 171.

10. But an angel *will* preach "an eternal gospel" to those who remain on earth in Revelation 14:6.

Chapter 9: Heaven's Heroes

1. Jerry Dykstra, "North Korea: A Clear and Present Danger to Christians," *Religion Today*, February 19, 2013, http://www.religiontoday.com/columnists/guest-commentary/north-korea-clear-and-present-danger-to-christians.html, accessed May 27, 2013.

2. C. S. Lewis, *The Complete C. S. Lewis Signature Classics* (New York: HarperCollins, 2002), 75.

Chapter 10: A Royal Cheering Section

1. Dinesh D'Souza, *Life After Death: The Evidence* (Washington, D.C.: Regnery, 2009), 53.
2. Lisa Miller, *Heaven: Our Enduring Fascination with the Afterlife* (New York: Harper, 2010), 186–187.
3. Miller, 189.
4. Doug Binder, "Prep runner carries foe to finish line," ESPN High School Sports, http://espn.go.com/high-school/track-and-xc/story/_/id/8010251/high-school-runner-carries-fallen-opponent-finish-line, accessed May 29, 2013.
5. Randy Alcorn, *Money, Possessions, and Eternity* (Wheaton, IL: Tyndale, 2003), 106.
6. John MacArthur, *The Glory of Heaven: The Truth about Heaven, Angels, and Eternal Life*, Second Edition (Wheaton, IL: Crossway, 2013), 66.

Chapter 11: Party Time

1. "The Day Billy Graham Found Christ," Billy Graham Evangelistic Association, http://www.billygraham.org/articlepage.asp?articleid=1843, accessed June 3, 2013.
2. "*It's a Wonderful Life* Quotes," Rotten Tomatoes, http://www.rottentomatoes.com/m/1010792-its_a_wonderful_life/quotes/, accessed June 3, 2013.
3. Stan Guthrie, *All That Jesus Asks: How His Questions Can Teach and Transform Us* (Grand Rapids, MI: Baker, 2010), 302.

Chapter 12: In the Twinkling of an Eye

1. Mark Hitchcock, *Could the Rapture Happen Today?* (Sisters, OR: Multnomah, 2005), 15.
2. "What is the meaning of 'twinkling of an eye'?" http://wiki.answers.com/Q/What_is_the_meaning_of_'twinkling_of_an_eye',' accessed June 6, 2013.
3. Greg Laurie, *Signs of the Times: What the Bible Says about the Rapture, Antichrist, Armageddon, Heaven, Hell, and Other Issues of Our Day* (Dana Point, CA: Kerygma Publishing, 2010, 2011).

Chapter 13: Here Comes the Judge

1. J. I. Packer, *Concise Theology: A Guide to Historic Christian Beliefs* (Wheaton, IL: Tyndale, 2001), 262–263.
2. C. S. Lewis, *The Great Divorce* (New York: HarperOne, 2009), 75.
3. Warren Wiersbe, *The Bible Exposition Commentary: Old Testament Wisdom and Poetry* (Colorado Springs, CO: Cook Communications, 2004), 495.

Chapter 14: Heaven's Rewards

1. Jason Mandryk, *Operation World: The Definitive Prayer Guide to Every Nation*, Seventh Edition (Colorado Springs, CO: Biblica, 2010).
2. Randy Alcorn, *The Law of Rewards: Giving What You Cannot Keep to Gain What You Cannot Lose* (Wheaton, IL: Tyndale, 1989, 2002, 2003), 18.
3. Randy Alcorn, *Heaven* (Carol Stream, IL: Tyndale, 2004), 443.
4. C. H. Spurgeon, "Watching for Christ's Coming," No. 2302, Metropolitan Tabernacle Pulpit, http://www.spurgeongems .org/vols37-39/chs2302.pdf, accessed June 12, 2013.

Chapter 15: Christ's Resurrection — and Ours

1. C. S. Lewis, *The Complete C. S. Lewis Signature Classics* (New York: HarperCollins, 2002), 427–428.
2. Randy Alcorn, *If God Is Good: Faith in the Midst of Suffering and Evil* (Colorado Springs, CO: Multnomah, 2009), 201.
3. Quoted in GoodReads.com, http://www.goodreads.com/quotes/ tag/frodo, accessed June 14, 2013.
4. Quoted in "Greg's Blog," http://blog.greglaurie.com/?p=1699, accessed June 14, 2013.
5. Wilbur M. Smith, *The Best of D. L. Moody: Sixteen Sermons by the Great Evangelist* (Grand Rapids, MI: Baker, 1971), 199–200, quoted in "Heaven and Chicago," *The Electronic Encyclopedia of Chicago* (Chicago: Chicago Historical Society, 2005), http://

www.encyclopedia.chicagohistory.org/pages/2399.html, accessed June 14, 2013.

6. E. M. Bounds, *Heaven—A Place, a City, a Home*, http://www .dailybread.com.au/e-books/EM_Bounds/Heaven%20-%20 A%20Place,%20A%20City,%20A%20Home.pdf, 6, accessed June 14, 2013.

7. N. T. Wright, *Surprised by Hope: Rethinking Heaven, the Resurrection, and the Mission of the Church* (New York: HarperOne, 2008), 95.

8. First definition, *The Free Dictionary*, http://www .thefreedictionary.com/city, accessed June 14, 2013.

9. "88 Hours Non-Stop," Judaism Online, SimpleToRemember .com, http://www.simpletoremember.com/articles/a/bird-facts/, accessed June 14, 2013.

10. John 14:5-6.